TWAYNE'S WORLD AUTHORS SERIES
A Survey of the World's Literature

SPAIN

Janet Pérez, Texas Tech University

EDITOR

Julián Marías

TWAS 642

Julián Marías

JULIÁN MARÍAS

By ANTÓN DONOSO
University of Detroit

TWAYNE PUBLISHERS
A DIVISION OF G. K. HALL & CO., BOSTON

Published in 1982 by Twayne Publishers,
A Division of G. K. Hall & Co.
All Rights Reserved

Printed on permanent/durable acid-free paper and bound
in the United States of America

First Printing

Library of Congress Cataloging in Publication Data

Donoso, Antón.
Julián Marías.

(Twayne's world authors series. Spain ; TWAS 642)
Bibliography: pp. 160-167
Includes index.
1. Marías, Julián, 1914–   . I. Title. II. Series.
B4568.M374D66   196'.1   81-6427
ISBN 0-8057-6486-0   AACR2

To my parents

Contents

About the Author

Antón Donoso holds the Ph.D. in Philosophy from the University of Toronto (1960). He has taught in the University of Detroit since 1959, where he presently is Professor of Philosophy, specializing in philosophical anthropology and social philosophy. In 1964 he was Fulbright Lecturer on "North American Thought" to Argentina. He is the author of articles, reviews, and abstracts in various anthologies and journals, including *The Predicament of Modern Politics, University of Detroit Law Journal, Revista Jurídica de la Universidad de Puerto Rico, Vanderbilt Law Review, International Philosophical Quarterly, The Personalist, Philosophy Today, Journal of the History of Philosophy, Proceedings of the American Catholic Philosophical Association, Conference on Developing Teaching Materials on Latin American Thought for College Level Courses, Bibliography of Philosophy, Américas, Filosofía,* "Anais do VIII Congresso Interamericano de Filosofía," *Los Ensayistas, Hispania,* and *Studies in Soviet Thought.* His interest in Spanish-language philosophical thought grew out of a study of the differences in response to European ideas between North America and Latin America. He is one of the founders of the Society for Iberian and Latin American Thought and is Assistant Editor for Spanish and Portuguese language journals for the *Philosopher's Index* of the Philosophical Documentation Center of Bowling Green State University, Ohio.

Preface

On an afternoon in early September 1963 a man sat next to me on a bus. We were participants in the Thirteenth International Congress of Philosophy, returning to our hotels from an exhibit of colonial era manuscripts and incunabula at the Library of the Universidad Autónoma de Mexico. For the first part of the trip he talked with an elderly couple across the aisle. He looked familiar, and soon I recalled having seen his photograph in some of the books I had purchased the previous summer in Madrid. After the conversation had terminated, I asked him: "Are you Julián Marías?" The man was he. I related that I had purchased the volumes of his *Obras* as I had heard he was the foremost interpreter of José Ortega y Gasset, but had not consulted them yet since I had only begun to read Ortega in depth that summer.

We talked briefly about the congress and about the beauty of Mexico, as it was the first visit to that country for both of us. He learned that my favorite Spanish city was Seville, and shared with me his discovery that the tiny plazas in a certain section of Mexico City looked like those in Andalusia. He was happy to be able to photograph them. (Later I was to read that photography was one of his hobbies, as well as searching out old books.) In parting he thoughtfully gave me his address in case I would have any questions concerning his writings.

Over the years my interest in Ortega grew, and I reviewed a number of Professor Marías's works when they appeared in English translation. My colleagues kept this in mind and Professor Richard Lineback of the Department of Philosophy of Bowling Green State University (Ohio) thoughtfully invited me there on two of the occasions Professor Marías visited the campus to lecture and conduct a seminar. Professor Gerald Kreyche of the Department of Philosophy of De Paul University (Chicago) did the same when Professor Marías delivered two lectures there. At a luncheon in Professor Marías's honor Professor Robert Lechner of the same department, and editor of *Philosophy Today*, suggested that I write an article on his contribution to philosophical anthropology. The article never appeared, and instead has grown into the present book.

The series in which this study appears necessitates that all the works of an author be covered, more than I would have included had I devoted a book to my original interest in Professor Marías's thought. In preparing this study, however, I have come to realize that what I thought was incidental matter leads up to that in which I am primarily interested, namely, Professor Marías's theory of the empirical structure of human life. One can see the theory gradually emerge from Professor Marías's biography, for, like Miguel de Unamuno and José Ortega y Gasset, his two greatest sources of inspiration, it is impossible to separate Julián Marías's writings from his life (chapter 1). His theory of philosophy as "responsible vision" enables Professor Marías to examine human life as the fundamental reality with which we experientially come in contact (chapter 2). In analyzing human life, constituted by being "I and my circumstances," Professor Marías came to realize, over a period of a quarter of a century, that there was an intermediate reality between those (essential) characteristics which we attribute to human life in general and the concrete (accidental) biographical reality that constitutes each particular human life. It is to this intermediate reality that he gave the name empirical structure, signifying as it does those characteristics human life has, as a matter of empirical fact rather than of logical necessity, on this planet (chapter 3). Human life's essential circumstantiality not only implies that we co-live with other humans (society), but that our co-living takes place with people of various generations (history) subject to partially different binding observances (chapter 4). Concrete forms of co-living can be seen only by carefully analyzing our impressions of various societies, both domestic and foreign, especially as manifested in their cities (chapter 5). The primary mode in which Professor Marías has presented the fruits of his personal experience has been through philosophical theory, expressed in a literary manner such that it preserves the "dramatic structure" of human life. Indeed, the theory that is philosophy becomes "incarnate" only in its literary form (chapter 6).

I am more convinced than ever that Professor Marías's theory of the empirical structure of human life is his major contribution to theory, a source for much further fruitful philosophizing. His consideration of long neglected or ignored aspects of human living, such as sex and age, places Professor Marías on the very frontiers of philosophical anthropology. In so philosophizing Professor Marías has taken as his principal mentor José Ortega y Gasset, who was one of those philosophers in the early years of our century who attempted to discover a middle ground between the excesses of rationalism and empiricism. Ortega's resulting "ratio-vitalism" maintains that the reality of human life is the object of philosophizing, placing the position, if I may speak very generally, within the Continental European movement of phenomenology (interested primarily in person and "existential" themes) and at odds with the Anglo-American movement of analysis (interested mainly in logic and language). These movements are not, by any means, mutually exclusive, and if Professor Marías's theory of language were developed further, it would do much to bridge the present chasm between them.

A philosopher's ultimate contribution depends, in part, on the willingness of others to spend time studying his thought so as to adopt it as their starting point in further consideration of the themes and directions he introduced. And, what is more important for the history of philosophy, these "others" must acknowledge him as their source and inspiration. In the case of Professor Marías there are beginning to appear those who so acknowledge him. He is, however, at a great disadvantage. Since Professor Marías's professional life has been lived in more than one field, professional philosophers are either unfamiliar with his work or consider it (mistakenly) as a commentary on that of Ortega. Accordingly, the next step must include an effort to give Professor Marías's theories the exposure to critical discussion they merit. Hopefully, this study is a step in bringing Professor Marías even closer to the English-reading public than has the translation of many of his works.

Limitation of space has prevented me from discussing in detail the relationship of Professor Marías to Ortega, including his interpretation of his mentor's thought. Accordingly, I have granted Professor Marías his contention that he is the heir of Ortega, his most authentic interpreter. Most certainly I agree with him that he is unintelligible without Ortega, yet irreducible to Ortega. However, Professor Marías is very much his own person. Sometimes I think that if he had spoken less of Ortega, he would have been criticized less by his Spanish colleagues. This, however, would have been "out of character" for him. At any rate, Professor Marías can neither be praised for the insights of Ortega nor blamed for what others—including myself—judge to be shortcomings of position or expression in Ortega. And, this despite Professor Marías's assertion that during Ortega's last decade of life he referred to his philosophy as "ours"—his and Professor Marías's—implying that Professor Marías not only had understood and interpreted him correctly, but that Professor Marías's development of Ortega's thought would be what Ortega himself would have approved. This statement has brought criticism upon Professor Marías from two fronts: those who find Ortega's position unacceptable, especially incompatible with Catholicism as understood in Spain; and those who disagree with Professor Marías's interpretation of Ortega, however sympathetic they may be toward Ortega himself. The topic, obviously, is sufficiently complex to warrant a separate book and, consequently, I have merely pointed it out.

The subject of this book continues to be as active as ever, at an age when most people are retiring, criss-crossing the Atlantic between Spain and the United States and/or Latin America. Since my manuscript was completed, Professor Marías has been awarded additional honorary doctorates (three in Argentina in 1980, for example), has had a session of the American Association of the Teachers of Spanish and Portuguese dedicated to his thought (at its sixty-second annual meeting in San Juan, Puerto Rico, in 1980), and has been appointed to a newly created chair of Spanish philosophy in the Universidad Nacional de Educación a Distancia in Madrid. His inaugural lecture was delivered on 18 October 1980, the twenty-fifth anniversary of the death of his mentor and friend, José Ortega y Gasset, after whom the chair was named. The appointment constitutes Professor Marías's first official academic position in his own country. As this study goes to press I have had word from Professor Marías that he has completed a fourth book on contemporary Spain. What I had thought would remain a trilogy will now be a series with the publication of *Cinco años de España* [Spain's Five Years]. Moreover, two additional volumes of his *Obras*, 9 and 10, will be appearing shortly and will include works previously unpublished in book form.

In presenting Professor Marías's contributions I have given the sources also in English, whenever available, so that those of my colleagues in professional philosophy who cannot read Spanish might have access to the context. (All translations are my own.) In this way I hope to encourage discussion and critique in wider professional circles than are now familiar with his work.

Professor Marías has been as helpful as his busy schedule permitted in preparing this study. Unfortunately, the times when we were both free did not often coincide, which I regret because all I managed to speak to him about were biographical matters. Professor Antonio Rivares of Texas Christian University and Professor Cecilia Silva de Rodriguez, then of North Texas State University, generously gave of their hospitality to facilitate my longest personal meeting with Professor Marías, when he was in Fort Worth to deliver a week of lectures during late April 1979. Professor Michael A. Weinstein and Mr. Joseph Rubin kindly shared their unpublished reflections on Professor Marías's position as it bears on their respective fields, political philosophy and psychology of the person. I wish to thank them, as well as all the publishers who granted permission to quote from material by and on Professor Marías, especially to José Vergara of Revista de Occidente, S.A. Above all, Professor Harold C. Raley of the Department of Spanish of the University of Houston extended to me more consideration and help than I could have dared hope for, including a copy of the manuscript he had just completed on Professor Marías. Mr. Paul Zancanaro kindly, and patiently, read the manuscript in its two drafts (the first was over one hundred pages too long), and offered his valuable advice on summarizing as well as on style and clarity. The result, of course, is my sole responsibility.

ANTÓN DONOSO

University of Detroit

Chronology

1914   17 June, Julián Marías Aguilera born in Valladolid.

1919   Moves to Madrid. Attends Instituto del Cardinal Cisneros (secondary school).

1931   Enters both Faculty of Sciences and Faculty of Philosophy and Letters, University of Madrid.

1932   Becomes student of Ortega. Remains in Faculty of Philosophy and Letters.

1933   Tour of Mediterranean sponsored by Faculty. Excerpts from diary published the following year.

1934   Speaks with Unamuno at International Summer School in Santander.

1936   Graduates from University of Madrid in spring.

1937   Mobilized into Army of Republic during Civil War.

1939   1 April, Franco declares Civil War at end. Imprisoned for three months during summer.

1940   Completes *Historia de la filosofía* [History of Philosophy]. Begins private courses in Aula Nueva (until 1948).

1941   Refused his doctorate in philosophy by University of Madrid for political reasons. 14 August, marries Dolores Franco Manera (five sons born to couple).

1943   *Miguel de Unamuno.*

1947   Awarded Fastenrath Prize from Royal Spanish Academy for *Miguel de Unamumo. Introducción a la filosofía* [Reason and Life: The Introduction to Philosophy].

1948   Founds, with Ortega, the Instituto de Humanidades (lasts for two years).

1949   *El método histórico de las generaciones* [Generations: A Historical Method].

1951   Awarded doctorate from University of Madrid with original dissertation, already published (1941) as *La filosofía del Padre Gratry* [The Philosophy of Father Gratry]. Travels to Hispanic America and the United States for the first of many trips (has taught and lectured at Wellesley, Harvard, Yale, U.C.L.A., the universities of Puerto Rico, Oklahoma, and Indiana, and countless other institutions).

1952 Begins many years of teaching American and other foreign students in Spain.

1953 Elected member of International Institute of Philosophy (Paris).

1954 *Idea de la metafísica* [Idea of Metaphysics] and *Biografía de la filosofía* [Biography of Philosophy].

1955 *La estructura social* [The Structure of Society].

1956 *Los Estados Unidos en escorzo* [The United States in Brief], which had appeared in Spanish newspapers, in which he was permitted to publish after 1951.

1960 *Ortega I. Circunstancia y vocación* [Ortega: Circumstance and Vocation], written with a Rockefeller Foundation Grant while visiting professor at University of Puerto Rico (1956). Elected member of Hispanic Society of America and International Society for the History of Ideas (New York). Founds and directs Seminario de Estudios de Humanidades in Madrid with grant from Ford Foundation to study social structure of Spain.

1961 *Imagen de la India* [Image of India].

1964 June, awarded first John F. Kennedy Prize for intellectual achievement by North American Studies Institute of Barcelona. 15 October, elected member of Real Academia Española (Royal Spanish Academy).

1965 20 June, delivered inaugural address in Real Academia Española on "La realidad histórica y social del uso lingüístico" [The Historical and Social Reality of Linguistic Usage].

1966 *Meditaciones sobre la sociedad española* [Meditations on Spanish Society], *Consideración de Cataluña* [Considerations of Catalonia], and *Nuestra Andalucía* [Our Andalusia].

1968 *Análisis de los Estados Unidos* [Analysis of the United States] and *Israel: Una resurreción* [Israel: A Resurrection].

1970 *Antropología metafísica* [Metaphysical Anthropology].

1971 Awarded Juan Palomo Prize for *Antropología metafísica*. Director of Summer School in Soria, organized by Centro de Estudios Sorianos (Center of Sorian Studies).

1972 Awarded Gulbenkian Essay Award from Academy of the Latin World (Paris) for *Antropología metafísica*.

1976 *La España real* [The Real Spain], first of trilogy on Spanish social conditions. Awarded Ramón Godó Lallana Prize for

Journalism for 1975–1976 for series of two articles on Dionisio Ridruejo published in *La Vanguardia* of Barcelona.

1977   Appointed senator by King Juan Carlos to Cortes (Parliament) to assist in drafting new constitution. *La devolución de España* [Spain Given Back to Itself], the second part of *La España real*. Wife Lolita dies in December.

1978   *España en nuestras manos* [Spain in Our Hands], third part of *La España real*.

1979   *Problemas del cristianismo* [Problems of Christianity]. Awarded León Felipe Prize for article "Una jornada muy particular" [A Very Special Day] on the Italian movie *Una giornata particolare*.

1980   *La mujer en el siglo xx* [Woman in the Twentieth Century]. Honored by a symposium on his thought at the Sixty-Second Annual Meeting of the American Association of Teachers of Spanish and Portuguese.

CHAPTER 1

Biography

I Spaniard

S HORTLY after the birth of Julián Marías Aguilera on 17 June, 1914 two events occurred that were key factors in the circumstances of his life: the appearance of José Ortega y Gasset's first book, and the assassination of the heir to the Austro-Hungarian throne. Marías was to adopt and expand the philosophic position first expressed in Ortega's *Meditaciones del Quijote* [Meditations on Quixote], while his life and work had to be undertaken in a world that has seen little peace since the shot fired in the Balkans.

The city of Marías's birth is the ancient one of Valladolid in Old Castile. It was there that his parents had met and were married, his father, Julián Marías de Sistac (1870–1949), coming from Aragon and his mother, María Aguilera Pineda (1874–1938), from Andalusia. Three sons were born to the couple: Pablo (1907–1910), Adolfo (1911–1930), and Julián. By his own account Julián was a precocious child, always curious and full of questions.[1] By continually asking what the various signs meant when he was taken out by his parents, he learned to read before beginning grammar school. By the age of seven he could read French well as the result of leafing through his father's French catalog of arms, comparing words and asking a few questions.

In 1919 the family moved to Madrid, of which city Marías considers himself a native in all respects except one. Unlike his wife and children, he does not pronounce the "ll" as "y." The capital city has grown dear to Marías so that whenever he goes away, be it to another part of Spain or out of the country, he always returns with joy. He retains fond memories of his secondary education at the Institute of Cardinal Cisneros, still feeling gratitude toward his teachers. The subjects toward which he was drawn were the sciences: mathematics, physics, and chemistry. However, Latin and

19

geography were his passion. He even felt a certain attraction toward philosophy although he knew little more than its name and a few facts. Since school was not too difficult for him, he had plenty of time to discover Madrid's nooks and crannies as well as to indulge in what seems to have always been one of his favorite pastimes, searching out and buying old books.

The young man had just passed his seventeenth birthday when he matriculated in both the Faculty of Sciences and the Faculty of Philosophy and Letters. After his first year, he decided to continue in Philosophy and Letters only. It was a time in which the country was becoming intensely politicized, extending even to Marías's Faculty or "College" within the University of Madrid. The majority of students, like most Spaniards, had had faith in the Second Republic when it was declared in 1931. But as violence grew and continued unchecked, the middle sectors of the political groups began to lose members to the extremists, so that by 1936 all that was lacking to set off a civil blaze was a spark. On 18 July the regular army revolted as part of the National movement. What was seemingly planned as a quick *coup d'etat* dragged out for three years amid much atrocity and many deaths. Shortly after Marías had received his first university degree he was mobilized into the Army of the Republic.

Marías was against both sides, against the Civil War itself as a remedy for the situation, thinking to this day it was the worst error of Spanish history, a criminal act foisted on the nation by extremists who were determined to prevent the majority from living in concord because they could not live with each other. Unfortunately the Spanish people permitted the nation to be torn asunder. Despite his attitude toward the war, Marías thought of the Republic as the legitimate political authority, worth defending even with its internal enemies. He was determined to do what he could to end the hostilities as quickly as possible, engaging in nonpartisan activities whenever possible. His rank was private, second class and his duties such that he is sure he did not contribute to the death of anyone. He did run certain risks, especially while assisting a companion who had charge of broadcasting government bulletins over shortwave radio. The two sent out clandestine appeals begging their fellow Spaniards to put an end to the fratricidal violence. Only the less rigorous supervision on the Republican side prevented them from being discovered before they ceased. During the last months of the war he offered his assistance to Julián Besteiro, a former professor of logic at the University of Madrid, and a past socialist president of the Cortes, in an attempt to bring about an honorable peace by preparing both sides for a peace of reconciliation that never came.

When the Civil War ended Marías says he thought Spain was exactly where it had always been: between the Pyrenees and the Straits of Gibraltar! The Spaniards had no one to blame but themselves, even for the foreign "assistance" which they had requested and accepted. After the hostilities ceased, Marías was arrested on suspicion of having Republican sympathies and held for three months in Madrid. He had been denounced by a former classmate, someone he had considered a good friend, a person who had first been a Republican and then had defected to the Franco zone. While in prison he held two jobs: teaching illiterates to read and do elementary mathematics, and teaching French in which he had become quite fluent. In addition, he delivered his first set of lectures to an audience of approximately one thousand, a few of whom would stop him on the street years later to remind him that they had been his auditors. The nonpolitical lectures were on the "History of Geographical Discoveries," including that of America.

In the meantime, preparations were being made for his trial, which could have ended in a long prison sentence or even death. It was clear that the prosecutor arbitrarily could admit witnesses and testimony so that the case for the accused was a foregone conclusion. But, knowing that certified testimony had to be admitted as part of the record, his fiancée, Dolores Franco Manera, obtained sworn statements on his behalf. What seemed to have been the key testimony on Marías's character, such that he never came to trial and was freed, was that of a man who held an important position in the Falange and who was a witness for the prosecution. When asked by the court why he was praising Marías since he was to be called as a witness against him, he responded that he thought he had been called simply to tell the truth.

The situation in which Marías found himself upon his release from prison is best summarized in his own words: "At that time, and for many years afterward, to be in Spain has signified to be an anvil or a hammer. My vocation never permitted me to be the second; my situation, moreover, brought me to the first."[2] He hastens to remind us that even the anvil has a degree of elasticity and is, to that extent, active. Marías had always considered himself a liberal, and he became more and more convinced of the validity of his position with the passage of the years under the Franco dictatorship. For Marías, a man has a right to make his own life and to live in his own country, as well as a right to reserve for himself a parcel of his life in which no authority has a right to interfere. In this sense, liberalism for him is primarily an attitude toward collective living and only secondarily a political position. He has characterized this attitude as "enthusiastic melancholy" because it combines a realistic recognition of the role of our emotions in life with a realization that we always fall short of our goals. Liberalism is the social organization of liberty, based as it it on a belief in man and human freedom. As such it is an instrument in man's search for happiness, involving a realistic acceptance of the human condition.[3]

Through all those years Marías was sustained by his close relationship with Dolores Franco Manera, his beloved Lolita. A member of a distinguished Spanish-Cuban family active in the arts and sciences, she attended the University of Madrid and studied philosophy and philology, becoming a disciple of Ortega, Américo Castro, Montesinos, and Salinas.[4] They met as students and shared an appreciation for Ortega's philosophy and its possibilities for authentic living, as well as a love of literature and gifts for writing and teaching. She taught in a number of private schools, in the summer session in Soria which Marías directed and for the programs in Madrid sponsored by Tulane and Bowling Green State Universities. The well-selected anthology entitled *España como preoccupación* [Spain as a Preoccupation] was edited by her.[5] Their marriage took place on 14 August 1941, the officiating priest being Manuel García Morente, their former teacher of philosophy and the dean of their Faculty. To them were born five sons, of whom four survive: Julián (1945), who died at the age of three and a half, Miguel (1947), Fernando (1949), Javier (1951), and Álvaro (1953).

Born on 31 December, 1912, Dolores Franco de Marías died in December 1977. The most fitting tribute to her and their marriage are the pages in her husband's *Antropología metafísica* [Metaphysical Anthropology] devoted to woman and love, as well as the expansion of these themes in *La mujer en el siglo xx* [Woman in the Twentieth Century]. It is clear that his insights and words spring from their close relationship, without which these studies would have been impossible. Especially memorable is the following passage:

Not many men have even a middlingly adequate idea of what a woman is. . . . Men do many things with women, but rarely think about them;

neither would this be enough: if man makes woman the "object" of his thought, he will never learn a word about her: only in the measure in which woman is *lived* as a specific woman can reason work upon her, can she be intelligible. For this reason, in the last instance, the man who "deals" with a woman knows more about her than the man who "studies" her, though innumerable key things still escape him. Were I to be asked for a concise expression, I would say that it is not a matter of thinking about women, but of thinking *with* them. And as thinking means to do what is necessary to know what to hold on to [in order to live], this means, in the most literal sense of the word, *living together*. Only when man and woman, each installed in his or her own sex, project toward each other, and together toward their dual personal vocation, is it possible for them to become mutually transparent; and only this dual life can set in motion the wholeness of vital reason [in its masculine and feminine forms].[6]

As early as the mid 1960s Marías was maintaining that the question being asked in Spain, "What will happen [after Franco]?," was the wrong one. Instead, he insisted, it should be: "What will we do?"[7] He had perceived that Franco's rule was too "personal" to be perpetuated by his followers *and* that the situation in Spain, especially the economic one, had changed so drastically that there was no comparison with pre–Civil War Spain. For all the illegitimacy of Spanish society—since Franco had no right to rule and did so only by sheer force—things were legally normal. Although foreign observers, especially Americans, viewed Spanish society as having no freedom, it was far from completely totalitarian. The small measure of economic freedom was critical, for it became the basis of other freedoms.

In order to contribute what he could to his countrymen's search for a direction, Marías decided to concentrate on Spain in his writings in the mid 1970s.[8] The result was his trilogy of personal reflections on what may prove to be the most decisive years in the entire history of modern Spain: *La España real* [The Real Spain], *La devolución de España* [Spain Given Back to Itself], and *España en nuestras manos* [Spain in Our Hands]. The series of essays was begun before Franco's death on 20 November 1975 and terminated after the new constitution had been drafted by the freely elected Constituent Cortes (Parliament), of which Marías was a member. King Juan Carlos was given the right to appoint forty members of the upper chamber, and he personally asked Marías to accept a senatorship. Despite Marías's dislike for politics, he agreed. He is sure that his criticism, which appeared in the daily press, of the original draft of the constitution helped to alter some of its worst features.

That to which Marías objected was the weakening of the Spanish nation in favor of regionalism.[9] Yet no one could accuse him of being a "nationalist." On the contrary, he says he is bothered by the superstition of nationalism in all its forms, especially in its twentieth-century manifestation of Fascism. As early as 1966, despite the censorship of the Franco regime that worked against regionalism of all kinds, Marías had called for respect for the differences of the Catalans, including freedom to use their own vernacular language. He pointed out that in some cases it was impossible to be a Spaniard "directly," but that this did not mean a Catalan was less Spanish. "The region is a marvelous, intimate reality, composed of daily ways of acting, of memories, of customs, of fine modulations, of plans; it is like a well-tuned instrument incorporated into an orchestra. There is no greater cruelty than a desire to destroy the regional reality so that it ceases to be or becomes something else," for by regional differences we have our roots in Spain.[10] What is to be avoided are the extremes of the nationalists who see regions as opposed to Spain and of the federalists who project their local problems over the entire nation.

The election of March 1979 saw the Union of the Democratic Center under Adolfo Suárez in the majority. Marías declined to run—all senators are elected under the new constitution—considering himself only a thinking citizen.[11] He credits Suárez and Juan Carlos with guiding the nation to a parliamentary monarchy under a democratic constitution. Suárez, premier during the immediate post-Franco years, slowly dismantled the totalitarian Falangist control, even with its own assistance. Juan Carlos rose to the occasion and acted like a legitimate monarch even before the free elections gave him legitimacy, thus meriting Marías's special respect. Both men guided Spanish society toward a liberalization before the elections so as to create public opinion, something nonexistent during the Franco years. Although Marías does not consider himself a monarchist, he believes the present form of government is the best for Spain.[12] He feels guarded optimism about Spain's future, despite the economic problems and the terrorism, both not indigenous to Spain but part of the international scene. Marías thinks that for the first time in history Spaniards have more possibilities, more resources, more choices than their imagination can handle. At long last Spain is in the hands of Spaniards, as men and women, even as old as Marías, have just now lost their "electoral virginity" and finally can have a voice in the future of their country.

II *Writer*

In English-speaking countries we often have to fill out forms that ask: "What is your occupation?" This simply inquires what we *do*. In Spanish-speaking nations the question on such forms, for instance on an application for a passport, is: "Qué es Usted?" ("What *are* you?"). When asked this question, Marías's response is: "I am a writer." It is not that he is who he is *and* happens to write. Marías exercises the activity of writing from the very depths of his personality, feeling himself fully a person only when writing. He is intimately connected not only to what he has written but to the very act of writing. In this sense being a writer, for him, is not merely having a profession, as may be the case with a carpenter, house painter, or salesperson, but having a vocation, of feeling a calling to engage in a certain activity, without which he would not consider himself to be who he is.[13]

On his flight to India in 1959 to attend an international philosophy conference, Marías recalled his long preoccupation with the subcontinent, and how it was linked to his early desire to be a writer. For it was during the summer when Marías turned ten, he tells us, that he made an important discovery, one that was to have far-reaching consequences in his life, namely, that the price of writing paper was not as expensive as he had always thought. He immediately purchased one hundred sheets of white paper and returned home with his treasure wrapped in green paper—he never forgot the color—full of plans and dreams. The following morning he sat himself in front of a small table, placed his sheets on it, and excitedly took out his pen and wrote: "Chapter 1." The youngster had begun to write a novel. Its setting was India, specifically the Bengal. That first package was followed by many more, and eventually gave way to a number of notebooks bound in shiny black oilcloth. Into them went adventure stories and more adventure stories, for he did not know how to end his novel. It seemed to grow indefinitely. Gradually he lost interest in the stories as the many incidents and characters took on comic shadings, even though the principal ones kept their heroism intact, despite the horrors and misfortunes that befell them. After a year his interminable manuscript was put aside. It was eventually lost, probably in the bombardment of his parents' home during the long seige of Madrid.

Marías has not attempted fiction since, although his outlines for some novels were favorably commented upon by certain novelists he knows. The possibility of attempting this genre has not left him completely, for he views the novel as a mode of philosophic knowledge, an observation he first made in conjunction with his study of Unamuno. Moreover, it would enable him to "concretize" his theory of human life to the fullest, illustrating what it is to live under the most specific circumstances possible. In this regard he considers the writing of novels as a possible next step in his vocation as a writer of theoretical works.

The first published work of the young Marías seems to have been excerpts from the travel journal he kept of a Mediterranean student cruise in the summer of 1933, a trip organized by the University of Madrid. Those reflections have the same purpose as his many later writings on his travels, what he has called his books on countries, namely, an attempt to let things speak for themselves by revealing their meaning through their ability to put us in contact with ourselves. The places we encounter show themselves to us in their depths, but we can interpret them only through our lives. As a result, the reflections of Marías reveal as much about his world as they do about him.

Looking back over his long career as a writer, Marías observed that his works have been very extensive but that he has never had to retract any of them, despite the fact that he does have many reservations about them. This is because they have always reflected his life and his world at the time. His attitude, he is certain, has no special merit, in all probability stemming from certain character traits he possesses: a tendency to think things through before plunging into them, a marked resistance to accept impositions, regardless of where they originate, a certain indifference toward what happens to be "in style," and an invincible repugnance toward the slogans or abstract solutions offered by political parties. As a result, the continuity in his opinions and attitudes is considerable, with variations due to changing circumstances.[14]

Even under Franco censorship Marías wrote with what he calls "interior freedom."[15] He resolved quite early that he would write as if there were no censorship. Deciding that he would not say everything he thought, he nevertheless was determined to think everything he said. What he wrote he truly held. "At the same time," he tells us in an essay reviewing his thirty years of intellectual life, "I decided not to do anything that I did not like. Not to write any book that I did not enjoy writing; the book itself may not have been to my liking because it was not good—and this is frequently the case with my books—but I have liked writing them."[16] Those who do things that they do not really like, simply because it is in style, are repulsed by their own works when they look back on them. "I had a terror that this might happen to me. One ought not to look back with repulsion, nor ahead with terror."[17] The so-called "self-censorship" was even disdained by Marías, a device by which writers were asked to police themselves and avoid certain topics. After all, Marías reasoned, he was not being paid to be a censor. More importantly, such self-censorship leads to the avoidance of thinking about certain things, an intrusion into one's private life that is repugnant to his liberal temperament. Inevitably certain articles would be rejected and returned. These Marías would put aside for a few weeks and resubmit, sometimes with the slightest, unessential modifications. Since the censorship was rather inconsistent, most items were eventually approved. Certain ones were forbidden publication in Spain and appeared in the foreign press. Marías still is certain that this attitude of his was the most effective. Others who disagreed with the regime did not publish at all, or if they did, said nothing about actual conditions so as not to be offensive. It was the policy of Marías to push censorship to its limits, always saying a bit more than was permitted in order to test the censors. Thus it was possible to be a nonconformist, a position that signifies an exercise of intellectual freedom, under an adverse situation.[18]

During Marías's years in the army he had been able to continue his writing, contributing to the Republican edition of *ABC*, *Hora de España*, and *Blanco y Negro*. (During his student years he had contributed to the journals *Cuadernos de la Facultad de Filosofía y Letras*, *Cruz y Raya*, and the well-known *Revista de Occidente*, founded and directed by Ortega.) The most fruitful essay he wrote during those years was on Unamuno and was later expanded into the book *Miguel de Unamuno* (1943), dedicated to his wife, for which he was awarded the prestigious Fastenrath Prize in 1947 by the Spanish Royal Academy. Upon his release from prison, since he had no prospects of obtaining a position teaching or writing for newspapers and journals, he turned—with the encouragement of his fiancée—to writing a book on the history of philosophy, using for his first draft her carefully taken notes from a course he had given in which she was a pupil. Revista de Occidente, the publishing house that Ortega had founded, agreed to bring it out, thus beginning what Marías considers his "adult life" as a writer for the general public. In 1948 *La Nación* of Buenos Aires invited him to contribute and he has done so regularly since. Essays of his have also appeared in *La Prensa* and *El Comercio* of Lima, as well as in *Novedades* of Mexico City, giving him quite a large public in Hispanic America, so that he keeps the region in mind when writing. In 1952 he was permitted by the regime to contribute to Spanish newspapers, although previously he had occasionally published in peninsular journals such as *Escorial, Leonardo,* and, later, *Insula.* Since 1962 he has written movie reviews for the *Gaceta ilustrada,* one of which, "Una jornada muy particular" [A Very Special Day], based on the Italian film *Una Giornata Particolare* and published in the 15 January 1978 issue, received the León Filipe Prize in 1979. He has contributed, likewise, to *La Vie Intelectuelle, Commonweal, Foreign Affairs, Confluence, The Dublin Review,* and the *New York Times.* The essays of his trilogy on Spanish affairs appeared originally in the newspaper *La Vanguardia* of Madrid beginning in 1974. The literary prize "Ramón Godó Lallana" was bestowed on him in 1976 for the first volume of the trilogy, as had been both the Juan Palomo Prize and the Gulbenkian Essay Award from the Academy of the Latin World of Paris in 1971 for his *Metaphysical Anthropology.* His tremendous and continuous literary output, especially during his younger years, made him feel that he was "drawing on account" from his later life. He manages to ward off exhaustion, he tells us, by undertaking more than one project at a time, resting from one by going to another.[19]

The manner in which a writer works has always been of interest to Marías, and he has sometimes included this information about his own works in their prefaces. A number of his books are collections of essays, his distinctive genre, previously published in newspapers and journals, most probably for financial reasons. Some were originally intended as books, while others "seem to grow" into such at a later date. However, the philosophically most important books were written as a whole, often during a single uninterrupted stretch. These include *Introducción a la filosofía* [Introduction to Philosophy], *Idea de la metafísica* [The Idea of Metaphysics], *El método histórico de las generaciones* [Generations: A Historical Method], *La estructura social* [The Structure of Society], and *Antropología metafísica* [Metaphysical Anthropology]. In the foreward to the last-mentioned book he informs us that, although the study was thought out over the course of some twenty years, the subject matter having been with him from the beginning of his philosophic exploration of human reality, he wrote it in sixteen unbroken months. The systematic nature of its theory and its literary form, he continued, demanded that it be written in a single mental movement, despite the fact that he had to move from place to place. He cautions that it must be read through rather than leafed through, for otherwise the dramatic structure of its form, corresponding to the dramatic structure of philosophic theory itself, will be mutilated. As a writer Marías has been especially sensitive to the problem of finding, or creating, the appropriate literary genre for his philosophy of human life.

Perhaps Marías was the most revealing of his manner of working in the "Prologue to the American and English Editions" of his first systematic treatment of philosophy, *Introduction to Philosophy*. One afternoon in the fall of 1945, we are informed, he sat down at his table with a sheet of paper and pen, and wrote for three or four hours.

By the time the sun had set, the paper was covered with writing, and I had the impression that I had in my hands the book that I intended to write. That sheet of paper contained a brief statement of its subject matter, in fifty lines, and an index of its chapters, which coincided in more than three fourths of the cases with what I actually had to write, with that which the reader has before him now. This means that the present book has a basic unity, which makes it advisable that it should be read in its entirety and without interruption. On that same day I began to write it, on the typewriter, as usual, in only one draft, with very few corrections, that went directly to the printers. On 20 January 1947, after fourteen months of uninterrupted work, I wrote the last page; for some weeks the printer had been setting up the book, which appeared before the end of the month.[20]

Continuing, Marías expressed his belief that the book's unitary mode of composition corresponded rigorously to its content. The unity of the book is not primarily that of a treatise but goes much deeper. It reflects the unity of the person, the biographical continuity of life itself. Once in possession of this, it was merely a matter for Marías to be faithful to it, letting the words express on paper the reality of human life. This alone is the meaning behind the book. As such the book is like a novel, without being a novel, in which contemporary Western man is the suprapersonal protagonist surrounded by secondary actors from other philosophical times.

On 15 October 1964 Marías was elected to the Spanish Royal Academy to fill the seat vacated by the death of Wenceslao Fernández Flórez. His inaugural address was delivered on 20 June 1965 and dealt with "La realidad histórica y social del uso lingüístico" [The Historical and Social Reality of Linguistic Usage], consisting of an application of the principle of binding observances in *The Structure of Society* to language. Given his ostracism by the Spanish state, the honor paid Marías by Spanish intellectual society was even greater than might at first appear.

As a writer of theory, as a philosopher and thinker, Marías views his role or mission as that of "verifying" the system of connective relationships that other writers merely present in portraying life in their works. Occasionally a previously hidden relationship might even be discovered. The writer, any writer, is the person who can propose to others new ways of living, new goals and aims in life. It is his function to know and explore human situations, to imagine their ins-and-outs, to show the attractiveness or value of the possibilities they offer, to establish a hierarchy for choice. The poet is able to create states of human spirit, of mind and feelings, that are sincere and authentic. These are able to draw our attention to those aspects of reality that would otherwise have been forgotten and lost to us, aspects that act essentially as "vitamins" for biographical life even as chemical vitamins are necessary for the biological life of the human animal. The novelist and dramatist, fiction writers, show the real and living connections or relationships of the world. They are our great educators and, at the same time, our great persuaders. They present to us, in a most efficacious manner, the reality of our historical and personal circumstances, so that we do not overlook the true riches of our life. Again, the writer of philosophic theory must "ground" or justify these links or connections, showing how they relate to human life itself, individually and collectively. Such has always been the task of writers, even if recently they have tried to impose on themselves others that they consider more lofty, but which are not because they deal in utopias based on a disrespect of reality, and lead to an impoverishment of human living by denying life as it really is.

III   *Philosopher*

By the time Marías had completed his first year at the University of Madrid, he was certain that philosophy was to be his lifelong central interest. His teacher that year, the eminent thinker Xavier

Zubiri, introduced Marías to two things for which he has always felt a gratitude of friendship: Ortega's philosophy and that of the Greeks. As a matter of fact, Marías had already had an introduction of sorts to Ortega. At the age of fifteen he had read Ortega's collection of essays entitled *Notas* [Notes]. Writing thirty years later, Marías recalls the feeling with which he first read Ortega, who seemed to have had *him* in mind, to have been talking directly *to him*. It was as if the door to a previously closed room had been opened. His young world had expanded.

One fall afternoon in 1932, in a room in the Valdecilla Pavilion of the old university, after having passed the trial of intellectual fire in the course by Zubiri, Marías met his new teacher for the first session of Ortega's course on the "Principles of Metaphysics according to Vital Reason."

When he entered the classroom I saw his countenance for the first time: serious and friendly, furrowed with deep wrinkles, looking somewhat like a manual laborer and a Roman emperor all at once. His eyes were clear and penetrating but without any harshness. They did not pierce like steel but like light. Now and again his face would light up with a happy and warm smile, with the lightning bolt of the grace of the Spanish. He began to talk. Perhaps his voice was the first revelation of who Ortega was; he was fully in it. Serious, and at times raucous, with dramatically low tones at the end of phrases; full of expressive shades of coloring, the words appeared to roll between his teeth, to leave his lips, destined precisely for each one of us in particular. Words were more fully words in his mouth than in the mouths of others. Not in vain had Ortega been one of the last two rhetoricians of our time—the other was Churchill. Ortega's hands, on the desk, were speaking their part with sober, elegant Mediterranean movements: gravity and grace joined in a gesture.
I never doubted that in many ways I was beginning a new stage in my life at that point. From that day, I never lost an opportunity to hear Ortega lecture; neither during the four years I was his student, nor in more recent years.[21]

These words were written twenty years later, at the time of Ortega's death in 1955. This may account for some of the emotion but not for any of the admiration, for Marías often wrote of his friendly affection for Ortega. He tells us, furthermore, that although he always listened to Ortega with devotion, it was also with a critical attitude. Ortega has to win Marías's intellectual assent. Above all, Ortega insisted that his students think, and keep on thinking, for themselves. But, the most personal lesson Marías seems to have learned from his mentor was that of continuous observation, the foundation of what Marías was to call his method of impressionism. Ortega, having perceived that the young Marías was rather introspective, cautioned him to open his eyes and continually fill his retina with fresh impressions because he could no longer do so when he grew older. "I felt the impact of his words; I got his point about the risk I was taking and forced myself, at first, to look and later looking became my delight: human faces—the only thing I noticed—people on the street, cities, countries, the most lowly things. [For] looking is two thirds of all philosophy that is not—in one way or another—scholastic."[22]

At the time of Marías's first course with Ortega, his professor was a member of the Cortes of the Second Republic. Ortega still held the chair of metaphysics, to which he had been appointed in 1910, and around him had been formed a group of admiring collaborators—the word "disciple" is too strong for most of them—that Marías calls "The School of Madrid." After an absence of three centuries, as Marías sees it, Ortega had recreated a philosophic milieu in Spain such that it matched in intellectual rigor the most scholarly work in any part of the world. Although remotely influenced by Miguel de Unamuno of the University of Salamanca, most of those associated with the group had been students of Ortega or, at least, students of his students. The positions held were often quite different, even in opposition. The "school" was radically Spanish in two senses: it was initiated by social circumstances in Spain, especially stemming from the country's defeat by the United States in 1898, and it was profoundly tied to the Spanish language, even creating a new philosophical vocabulary in Spanish where none had existed. Ortega had been the teacher of Manuel García Morente, while Ortega and Morente had taught Zubiri; the three had been the teachers of José Gaos, and Marías was the student of all four thinkers. Of this he is proud and grateful, never missing an opportunity to state that he studied at the University of Madrid when its Faculty of Philosophy and Letters, guided by García Morente as dean, was at a height of an intellectual rigor and academic freedom that it has never since regained.[23]

With the beginning of the Civil War Marías lost personal contact with Ortega, who had escaped to France where he soon faced dangerous surgery. From Paris Ortega went to Holland and then to Argentina (1939–1942). He sailed to Portugal with his wife and daughter, while his sons, who had stayed in Spain and joined

Franco's forces, ran the family publishing house. In 1940 Ortega had sent word from Argentina giving permission for the publication of Marías's *History of Philosophy*, without even having read it. Eight years passed before Marías saw him again, when Marías and Lolita journeyed to Lisbon. (He may not have gotten the required passport except for the quick thinking of the director of a Spanish cultural institute in Lisbon, who had the foresight to extend Marías an official invitation to lecture there.) In those eight years it was possible to exchange only two letters with his mentor. The first concerned the war, which Ortega was hesitant to discuss, recommending to Marías that "attitude of serenity that foreigners call 'Spanish gravity.' " The second, five years later, encouraged Marías to continue working despite his isolation from intellectual circles, calling his tactic of constant work the only right one for the times.[24]

During the visits to Lisbon, in 1944 and for two weeks again in 1945, Marías spent the time in almost constant association with Ortega: in long conversations, philosophical discussion, minute analyses of Marías's understanding of Ortega's books, and ". . . of the possibilities of a philosophy that Ortega began at that time to call 'ours.' "[25] This must have been a source of delight and encouragement to the young man. In the years that Marías had not had any guidance from his mentor, he had reread Ortega's books and the notes from his lectures. It was a key time in Marías's life as a philosopher, for he was formulating his own position through reflection on things and discovering that he was being drawn closer and closer to the truth and fecundity of Ortega's thought. Circumstances and personal problems pushed Marías, he contends, to the very center of Ortega's philosophy. This did not escape his mentor's notice, for years later Ortega wrote to Marías: "In reality you became my disciple *after* I ceased being [your] professor, in the years of my absence and of your own rethinking and maturation."[26]

Certaintly Marías considers himself a disciple of Ortega. But the word covers up the fact that Marías's discipleship does not exclude a profound influence, seemingly far removed from Ortega, by Unamuno. It likewise tends to obscure the fact that his relationship is a living and growing one that has included the application of Ortega's principles and philosophic method, as Marías understands them, to areas his teacher never considered. Nowhere is this more evident, as we shall see, than in his *Metaphysical Anthropology*. He called his first systematic treatment of philosophy, his *Introduction to Philosophy,* a "filial" one and dedicated the book to Ortega, by which term he meant

> . . . that it comes *from him* and that it moves in *another situation.* Intellectual genealogy is decisive, because intellectual life is lived in community; but in it, in contrast to everyday life, it is the son who recognizes the father. The son is not the father, nor can he be him, precisely because he *comes* from him, and can not reduce himself to him, because what is human is irreducible; the son comes from the father and goes toward himself; that is, he moves from his own proper level, and because of this faithfulness to a mentor, what can be called legitimate filiation, can not be other than an innovation. For this reason, the relationship between the thought of a man and that of his mentor can be stated in this way, which is valid for the relation of any philosophy with all past philosophy: inexplicable without it, irreducible to it.[27]

In 1945 Ortega returned to Spain. He lived in Madrid for long periods, traveling at home and abroad, with the government paying no attention to him and, supposedly, not interfering in his affairs. During those times, Marías says: ". . . our friendship became closer and closer and [our meetings] more and more frequent, our basic agreement even more profound, our discussions even more impassioned and interminable."[28] In 1948 they jointly founded the Institute of Humanities. In Marías's words: ". . . he generously included me [in its formation], availing himself of both our mutual identification and independence, our common 'having nothing to lose.' "[29] The venture lasted two years, and gave Marías the opportunity to present the series of lectures that constitutes his book *Generations: A Historical Method.*

Truly Marías had nothing to lose. A teaching position in a Spanish university was out of the question, not only for political reasons, since he had been imprisoned, but because of his adherence from his first book to Ortega's philosophy, which was being academically discouraged in Spain for religious reasons. From 1940 until 1948 he taught private courses in the New Classroom (*Aula Nueva*), a small institute founded by Marías and his wife, plus some of their friends, including the sons of Ortega. Among his students were many attending philosophy courses at the University of Madrid, where he had been refused the doctorate for political reasons. From 1952 he gave numerous courses for foreign students studying in Spain, especially Americans from Smith, Middlebury, San Francisco College, Mary Baldwin, Indiana, and, with the collaboration of his wife, Tulane.

His doctoral thesis, a study of the philosophy of God of the French priest Alphonse Gratry (1805–1872) had been published in spite of the fact that the degree was denied him. It was not until 1951, after the change of a key administrator, that Marías was approached by the university with an offer to award him the belated degree. He insisted that his thesis should be the original one, with an updated bibliography, and they agreed. Even his most widely used book, his *History of Philosophy,* that had filled a real gap and was eagerly sought after by students for its concise and clear presentation, was treated until then as if it did not exist. Indeed, there seems to have been a wall of hostile silence surrounding him, although a few at the University of Madrid, for example, the priests Juan Zaragüeta and Manuel Mindán, sometimes mentioned him in their classes, according to José Luis Pinillos, who was a student of philosophy at the university at that time.[30]

Marías had to go outside of Spain to become a university professor, usually to the United States.[31] An unexpected invitation from Wellesley College to act as Mary Whiton Calkins Visiting Professor for the academic year 1951–1952 led to many more trips. The summer afterward he taught at Harvard, then at the University of California at Los Angeles (1955), Yale University (1956), several times at the University of Puerto Rico, and he offered minicourses each fall term for a number of years at the University of Oklahoma and Indiana University. In addition to these major invitations, he accepted others for seminars and lectures throughout the United States, Hispanic America, and Europe. The major invitations, with the exception of Yale, were from the departments of Spanish and modern languages. The predominance of linguistic and analytic philosophy of various kinds in the departments of philosophy in the United States precluded many invitations from this source. Yale was an exception, especially at that time, for it offered its students a variety of positions to study. Despite the fact that he was offered a permanent position there, he chose to return to Spain.[32]

Earlier, when speaking of the School of Madrid, it was pointed out that its members had been remotely influenced by Unamuno. Certainly none of them could be said to have been his disciples; it is difficult to imagine Unamuno having a disciple, for his thought is essentially personal. For a student of philosophy his writings are baffling, as they claim to be "poetry," although they deal with what

have come to be considered philosophical themes since the advent
of the movement known as existentialism. Marías had first read
Unamuno in secondary school. He had not known him long or well,
having met him only during the International Summer School in
Santander in 1934, where he talked with him on various occasions
during a period of fifteen days, and heard him lecture. The news of
Unamuno's death reached Marías on New Year's Day 1937, on a
troop train loaded with volunteers from the famed International
Brigade.

It always has bothered Marías not to be able to understand
something, and he could not understand Unamuno's writings.[33]
During some free time in 1938 he decided to have it out with
Unamuno once and for all, the result leading to his award-winning
study, *Miguel de Unamuno* (1943). Like the spiritual cannibals that
we are, Marías devoured Unamuno and expanded his own personality.[34] The interpretation of Marías was that Unamuno was not a
philosopher in the strict sense of that word. Although his themes
coincide with the most essential ones of philosophy, Unamuno's
treatment is prephilosophic, inevitably linked to philosophy. Unamuno felt the problems of philosophy very strongly and very
accurately, but was unable to arrive at true philosophical activity.
Certainly Unamuno's works stand on their own as true literature.
By using poetic, novelistic, and dramatic means that cannot be
systematic, Unamuno filled his works with penetrating insights and
issues that need a philosophic method to draw out their theoretical
consequences.[35] Marías is certain that that method is provided by
Ortega. If Unamuno's insights focused on the issues that later
became Marías's questions, "Who am I?" and "What is to become
of me?," Ortega's discovery provided the means by which we can
theoretically attempt answers.

On 18 October 1955 Ortega, whom Marías was to call "my best
friend," died of cancer in Madrid at the age of seventy-two.[36]
Marías's interminable conversation with Ortega was interrupted—
not ended—for, in Marías's words: "As I believe in life everlasting,
I look forward to a never-ending conversation. And as I also believe
in the resurrection of the body, I hope to hear his affectionate voice
again and to feel his eternally friendly hand in mine."[37] There
followed an avalanche of obituaries and articles that briefly interrupted the attacks by the Catholic clergy and Scholastic philosophers on Ortega's thought. However, Ortega was given a Catholic
funeral, arranged by a priest-friend of the family, and the govern-

ment sponsored an official requiem. Adolfo Muñoz Alonso, director of the journals *Crisis* and *Augustinus,* challenged Marías's right to call Ortega "Spain's greatest philosopher" because Ortega has not covered the classical, and Christian, themes in philosophy: soul, world, transcendence, and God. The implication as regards Marías seems to be quite clear: Ortega's philosophy is incompatible with Catholicism and Marías, despite being a practicing Catholic all his life, is inconsistent in thinking that it is. In an essay written shortly after Ortega's death, Marías reminded Ortega's detractors that no one had lost his faith on account of Ortega. And, he added: "to me, personally, his friendship and teachings have served as an efficacious help in overcoming temptations coming from those quite other than he," which is more than Ortega could say about the Catholics who had been his own teachers. Furthermore, he reasoned, those who say that Ortega does not deal with God in his works forget the second commandment, that places upon us the obligation of not using the Lord's name without a reason, there being no universal necessity to bring God into a work on thought.[38]

Although all of Marías's works may be called philosophic, at least in the sense that they are based on philosophical principles operative and detectable below the surface and between the lines, he sees his key contribution to philosophy as *Metaphysical Anthropology.* It constitutes the last step in his effort to understand human life. Three works lead up to it, and together the four books may be called his major philosophical contribution. First came what happened to be also his first book, *History of Philosophy,* presenting the philosophic past and bringing us up to date. That was followed by *Introduction to Philosophy,* specifically devoted to philosophy as the theory of human life. Collective life was presented in *The Structure of Society,* while the view of human life in its empirical structure, as realized in "man," was given in *Metaphysical Anthropology.*

In the last book Marías tells us he "stumbled" on the problem of empirical structure, even though he did not see it with complete clarity, as early as 1947 and his *Introduction to Philosophy.* The problem was, specifically, whether we can pass directly from the analytical structure of human life, those general characteristics without which human life does not exist, to the biography of an individual man in trying to understand him philosophically. Marías suspected there was a missing link between the two, an intermediate stratum of reality that philosophers had overlooked in theorizing. While preparing his lectures on the theory of generations as a method of history, Marías discovered the precise difficulty. He soon (1952) expressed it in an essay on "La psiquiatría vista desde la filosofía" [Psychiatry Seen from Philosophy] and, later (1963), in "La estructura corpórea de la vida humana" [The Corporeal Structure of Human Life].[39] Since then it has been Marías's constant concern, and he dedicated an entire book, *The Structure of Society*, to studying it obliquely in the sphere of collective life. With *Metaphysical Anthropology* he attacked the question directly.

The existence of the empirical structure of human life is seen best when we realize that there is an entire stratum presupposed in any individual's biography, say that of Cervantes. A dictionary's listing of Cervantes gives a narration of his life that tells us when and where he was born, where he lived and traveled, what he wrote, when and where he died. It gives details like the fact that he lost the use of an arm in the Battle of Lepanto, married a woman named Catalina, wrote *El Persiles* [Persiles] in old age. But, the analytic or general theory of human life says nothing of having arms, being sexuated, or growing old. These must be assumed in his biography.[40] It was this zone of reality that Marías sought to expose, as no one quite had done in the past, by using Ortega's method of unveiling reality, the method of Jericho, of intellectually capturing the truth by an ever-narrower encircling of the target until its walls come tumbling down to reveal itself. This is what philosophy does— according to Julián Marías.

CHAPTER 2

Philosophy

I Origin and History of Philosophy

THE first question that requires our attention in discussing philosophy is: "Why did man begin to philosophize?" The response of Aristotle, the first of only a few to raise this fundamental query, can not be improved upon: awe! At first it was awe or astonishment of the strange things near at hand, but gradually this was extended to more fundamental, and important, things. Philosophy began the moment people ceased to circulate comfortably among everyday things and felt obliged to ask the question: "What is this?" This completely new attitude, which Marías calls a brilliant discovery, may be considered the theoretical, in contrast to the mythic, attitude. The previous mythic posture considered things to be powers or persons, benign or harmful, to be lived with or shunned, rather than simply as things having their own existence, properties, and meaning apart from men.

After the Greeks the question is: "Why do men continue to begin to philosophize?" The answer is the same: astonishment! Post-Hellenic man does not discover philosophy for humankind, but only for himself and his contemporaries. He, like his predecessors, can only philosophize when he feels an inexorable necessity within his concrete historical circumstances to do so. Each individual person of each succeeding generation must feel a need to know, of which philosophy is the only means of obtaining that knowledge, and he must opt for that way of knowing. In other words, he must have a genuine problem that can be approached only by philosophy. What complicates the issue is that we have abused the word "problem" in the last few centuries by calling every question a problem. Problems are precisely those questions with which we can no longer live peacefully, and which become obstacles in the sense that we feel obliged to pass to the other side of them by going through them,

39

rather than around them. These vital problems arise from the cracks in the system of accepted beliefs and ideas found in each person's circumstances.

The reigning belief in contemporary Western society is science. The sciences constitute a belief in the strict sense for the majority of Westerners rather than bodies of propositions thought out in a formal, intellectually rigorous fashion. These men are not able to prove or disprove anything scientifically, yet they believe it can be done and, what is more, base their lives on it. According to Marías, this belief exhibits strains because the individual sciences have no sufficient answers for the nucleus of basic, radical questions concerning life.[1] The sciences afford us certainty in regard to *some* things, precisely the things that are the objects of study in the respective sciences. At times the certainty of one science may even contradict that of another, as in the conflicting descriptions of a human from the sciences of physics, biology, and psychology. The sciences require a knowledge both to respect their autonomy and to arbitrate among them, giving a fundamental and universal certainty.

Such a total conviction is offered by religion, art—and since the Greeks—philosophy. The certainty of religion is a received one, given gratuitously by God to man through revelation. On the other hand, art and philosophy are attained by man through his own ingenuity, discipline, and effort. Art, unlike philosophy, does not "justify" itself, cannot account for itself, has no intrinsic evidence. Only philosophy constantly demonstrates its own validity by enabling us to live humanly. To the man who feels himself lost despite the certainties of science, who is "astonished" that science does not offer fundamental certainty despite his belief in it, philosophy offers a means to know radical—or fundamental—reality and to obtain radical certainty.

Since philosophy does not reign today, except in the negative sense that what reigns is the doubt that philosophy can fulfill its claim,[2] man cannot go to any socially accepted and living philosophy presently at hand (unless he is forced to do so, as in certain totalitarian societies). What is left is to go to the history of that traditional claim, to what philosophers have done for some 2,500 years. The history of philosophy shows us the "historical reason" for which there has been philosophy in each epoch, and why philosophy exists today. This appeal to the history of philosophy in trying to understand philosophy ". . . is as legitimate as it is indispensable, and only with it can we realize our purpose of approaching philosophy in its living and palpitating reality."[3] The history of philosophy is not merely a repertory of systems, a chronological enumeration of opinions, added one to another as in a collection, but is real history, a dramatic story, that exhibits a certain movement of the human mind in a total situation that is itself historical.

An adequate history of philosophy, if we are to make contact with life and the means to live with its problems, roots philosophy in the lives of those engaged in it, who are themselves grounded in their times—all of which must be viewed from our present situation as its essential actualization or fulfillment. As such, an authentic history of philosophy is neither a catalog of philosophical trends nor a treatment of problems that omits the historically concrete situations out of which they arose. Knowledge of the history of philosophy is the necessary, but not sufficient, pre-existing condition for the possibility of philosophizing. What is required, in addition, is the felt need to live with a vital problem as only philosophy can enable us.

The relationship of philosophy to its history is not like that of science, for example, to its own history. Science is one thing; its history is quite another. The two are independent so that science can exist, be understood and cultivated separately from its history. This is because science is the knowledge available at a particular moment of an object, its subject matter. Philosophy's "object" is itself; its problem is itself. This problem cannot be stated except according to the historical and personal situation in which the philosopher finds himself. This situation, in turn, is to a great degree conditioned by the philosophical tradition to which the philosopher belongs, whose roots are in still older ones going back to the very origins of philosophy. Thus, in every act of philosophizing the entire philosophic past is included. Every philosopher must keep one foot in the present situation, which dictates his concerns, and the other in the past, at the beginning, to show how his concern was treated in other situations.

That is, philosophy must establish and fulfill itself wholly in every philosopher, not in any manner, but in every philosopher in a unique way: the way in which he has been formed by all previous philosophy. Therefore, all philosophizing includes the entire history of philosophy, without which it neither would be intelligible nor, above all, could it exist. And at the same time, philosophy possesses no more reality than it achieves historically in each philosopher.[4]

This essentially inseparable connection between philosophy and its history is due to the fact that philosophy as a human activity is historical, and the activity cannot occur without its past being a dimension of it. Yet philosophy is never just its history; the present situation with all its obstacles to living prevents that. Philosophy does not exhaust itself in any one of its systems but consists of the "true" history of all philosophic systems, by which Marías means the story of how no system can exist independently but requires and involves all previous systems, out of which it emerges as the adequate or "true" response to contemporary problems. This is why each system of philosophy achieves its maximum reality, that is, its full truth, only outside itself—in the thought of those philosophers who are to inherit, absorb, and develop it (as Marías did with the thought of Ortega, Zubiri, and Unamuno, and as they did with the thought of still others, etc.). To say that philosophy is essentially historical only means that all philosophizing originates from the totality of the past and projects itself toward the future, thus advancing the history of philosophy. The history of philosophy is not merely a process but can be a progressive process (as Marías sees in the case of Ortega and many others).

There is no surer way of remaining faithful to the historical nature of philosophy than to survey its history. In such a view we readily see that philosophy is not something that exists, but rather is something that is happening, is making itself. It is precisely this that Marías attempts to illustrate in his *History of Philosophy*. As he views it, philosophy has a "discontinuous structure." There have been long periods of time that were like great gaps in philosophical activity. In these periods man was reduced to trivial meditation, spending his time commenting on and interpreting earlier works. This is in sharp contrast to those periods in which brilliant philosophers appeared in close succession. Examples of these include the fifth and fourth centuries B.C. (Parmenides, Socrates, Plato, Aristotle), the thirteenth and fourteenth centuries (Bonaventure, Aquinas, Duns Scotus, Roger Bacon, Eckhardt, Occam), the seventeenth and early eighteenth centuries (Descartes, Malebranche, Spinoza, and Leibniz on the Continent and Francis Bacon, Hobbes, Locke, Berkeley, and Hume in England), the last half of the eighteenth and the first third of the nineteenth centuries (Kant, Fichte, Schelling, and Hegel), and the early twentieth century (Dilthey, Husserl, Heidegger, and Ortega). The periods of philosophy's waning, when it loses momentum and becomes trivial, are often ones in which the ideas of the previous periods are disseminated among wider and wider circles.

Greek philosophy, according to Marías, had a purity and original-ity superior to all that was to come later, because it had no philosophic tradition behind it. It emerged directly from the Hel-lenic belief in a world that had always existed, was endowed with potentiality, was composed of a multiplicity of changing things defined by opposites, and was intelligible because of being ordered according to laws. The coming of Christianity marked a new era. It would be wrong to speak of Christianity as a philosophy and also of a Christian philosophy. What existed was the philosophy of Chris-tians *as Christians*. In other words, there was a philosophy shaped by the beliefs of the Christian situation, from which particular philosophers began to philosophize. These beliefs included an entirely new idea of the world, namely, its creation. Whereas the Greeks did not question the being of all things, this was exactly what the Christians found strange and in need of an explanation. For the Greeks "being" meant to be there; for the Christians it meant not being nothingness. The being of the world was inter-preted through the being of God. Thus, Christianity affected philosophy in a decisive manner; its religious belief posed the philosophical problem of creative and created being. The result was Scholasticism.

Western man's religious situation, along with his entire sociopol-itical organization, became problematic by the end of the Middle Ages. In what we call the Age of the Renaissance, theology began to rely less on philosophy, becoming more mystical, so that philoso-phers turned reason to nature and man. The Empire was dissolving into nations, giving rise to a philosophical preoccupation with the state, but completely ignoring the historical dimensions of this reality. With the renewed interest in the humanism of antiquity, the era quickly lost its autumnal character, due to the medieval religious consciousness of the Second Coming, and took on the air of a springtime reawakening. But, Renaissance philosophy was too un-disciplined and is negligible in the story of philosophy's movement. All, however, was not anti-Scholasticism. A less visible but more profound continuation of the authentic philosophy of the Middle Ages achieved its full maturity, its ultimate consequences, with a new idea of nature in the seventeenth century. Expanded trade and exploration in the fifteenth and sixteenth centuries had already prompted modifications of traditional philosophy by certain theologians who were "men of their times."

By the time we reach the eighteenth century, the epoch of the Enlightenment, philosophical speculation on the metaphysics of the previous century had ended. The ideas of the great European minds of the seventeenth century became less precise, really superficial and trivial images of themselves, as a result of the effort to popularize these ideas by a group of able and ingenious writers who ironically insisted on calling themselves *"philosophes."* These ideas penetrated the atmosphere so completely that they were taken for granted. By then Europe had changed into a different world, with the scene set for that radical alteration of history known as the French Revolution. Soon the nineteenth century was upon us. Actually nineteenth-century philosophy did not begin until the second third of that century, when idealism became spent. It was at that time that the emphasis on science began to grow to such proportions that philosophy was overwhelmed and almost disappeared.

Our own age thus finds itself in a situation of having to create a new philosophy, including having to show both the necessity for and possibility of it. This new philosophy, especially its metaphysics, will have to be based on authentic, fundamental reality. Toward the end of the nineteenth century, certain philosophers, all ignored or misunderstood by their contemporaries, led the way. In their thought can be detected a return to tradition and a discovery of human life as the subject matter of philosophy. Because of them, really two separate groups, philosophy began to regain its full dignity at the beginning of the present century. As a result, a new state of philosophical activity became possible. Of the philosophers engaged in this activity, it was Ortega who stood out as bringing together the two groups through basing his metaphysics on a description of human life as the radical reality. Marías clearly sees himself as continuing this philosophic movement, and thus as incorporating into his philosophizing the entire history of what came before him.

II   *The Biography of Philosophy*

In order to understand the meaning of the deepest level of the history of philosophy it is necessary to focus our attention more directly on what philosophy has meant from Greek times to our own. It will be seen that, aside from any differences of content, what has been meant by philosophy has not always remained the same. The men who have philosophized have done so in quite different ways and with quite diverse purposes in mind. This is the direct result of their individually unique lives, embracing distinctive aims in dissimilar situations. This human activity of philosophizing partakes of the lives of those who engage in it and, for this reason, can be called a "biography."

If we cast our glances backward to the earlier days of philosophy and rest them on Plato, the first Greek whose writings have been preserved, and ask ourselves what was the task facing him as he set out to philosophize, the changing meanings of philosophy will be seen clearly. By Plato's time the term "philosophy" had been in use for two hundred years. From the first only a few individuals had philosophized; the others continued as before, not finding wanting the old way of appealing to myths to deal with things. The new way was a means of reaching and dealing with the latent reality hitherto revealed exclusively in oracles and sacrifices, of unveiling what was formerly darkly concealed to man. In this sense philosophy "... does not *have* a method but rather *is* itself method."[5] What was being sought was the "consistency" of things, affairs, one's fellow men, and, especially, oneself—all in order to live with them, to depend on their acting always in a certain manner. To do this definitions were seen to be needed to capture the "reality" of each thing. This led Plato to deny that the consistency of things resides in things themselves (which Aristotle, his pupil, will later dispute). Since things appear to be the opposite of consistent, philosophy became a denial that reality is what it is believed to be. It became primarily a personal matter rather than a science; it was a reality experienced by man rather than a mass of propositions. It was this vision of reality that Plato sought to share with his pupils, including Aristotle, so that they could find things on their own.

In the years following Aristotle's death a change of attitude occurred toward philosophy. It was understood not so much as "first philosophy" or metaphysics that studies being as such, but rather as the secondary disciplines of logic, physics, and ethics. This was the view of the Stoics, whose influence lasted for five hundred years, and of all Romano-Hellenic philosophy. None of those philosophers lived the theoretic life of the metaphysician but were men of action, including Seneca and the Emperor Marcus Aurelius. The men who found Stoicism attractive were seeking something quite different from those who found Platonism and Aristotelianism satisfying. To them philosophy was not a science in the sense of theoretic knowledge whose object is the contemplation of the truth of things, but a guiding art to direct life. This involved a fundamental change in the meaning previously given to the term. Philosophy was not a response to a crisis of knowledge by a few individuals, but an answer to the problem of insecurity in a world undergoing social and political change to many people. It had ceased to be the patrimony of the few.

When we turn to the Christian era we find that philosophy once again exhibits its inseparability from the circumstances from which it arises, its link to the man who conceives it, and its meaningfulness within the situation in which it was created. Each time man discovers he must philosophize ". . . it is because his circumstances present some problem, his entire situation is problematic, and in order to live in it he must philosophize."[6] It is necessary to discover the precise reasons why men philosophize or their philosophy is incomprehensible. In the medieval world this reason was the desire to determine or "demonstrate" the truth, within several given opinions or interpretations, of how to live a religious life. Religious beliefs were part of the social structure of that world. Philosophy at the time had a link to religion that it had never had before or since. Scholasticism, the intellectual creation of a Christian world, was both a philosophy and a theology.

It was only during the Renaissance, void as far as philosophy is concerned, that Scholastic philosophy came into its own as an independent activity. Paradoxically, this independence came largely from the hands of a theologian, Francisco Suárez, who insisted he could not do theology without a firm grounding in metaphysics. Instead of merely commenting on previous writings, he set about to rethink them in the light of things in their new historical circumstances (international law, nationalism, Reformation, and Counter Reformation, etc.). His system would have been truly outstanding and influential except for the omission of one historical fact, the new mathematical physics—for which we must wait until Bacon and Descartes. Yet, while other outstanding minds, for example, Michel de Montaigne, were lost in the dense forest of opinions and were heading inexorably toward skepticism, Suárez was thinking these opinions through for himself, always—it must be added—in view of things, to arrive at the "true" ones without favoring any author in particular. In doing this he attempted to reconstruct what various authors tried to say from what they actually did say, delving into the context of their statements. This was a new method, in which natural theology was separated from supernatural theology, a rebellion against rote memorization, morbid delight in terminology and excess commentaries. Suárez wrote the first *treatise* on metaphysics, introducing that new literary genre, for even Aristotle's work was merely a series of more or less independent studies.

For the two or more centuries of the Renaissance, Europe needed a new kind of knowledge about things, something most minds failed to see. What efforts were made proved to be of no avail until Descartes. The topics of philosophy in the new historical circumstances were the world and the mind that conceives of that world mathematically. No help could be expected from the Scholastics, for they lent a deaf ear, tending to hold that all important questions already had been resolved. Descartes's attempt to reach the truth, although based on the general postulates of medieval philosophy and unintelligible without Christianity, was grounded in his conviction that he had no convictions (truth). Descartes was dominated by a fear of error rather than by a zeal for the knowledge of truth, despite the fact that for him philosophy is the search for truth by means of man's natural powers.

The philosophy of Descartes must be distinguished from Cartesianism, the product of the various philosophers he inspired to elaborate their own thought rather than repeat his. However, his major problem was theirs: the communicability of substances, that is, how it is possible for one kind of reality (matter, the world) to influence the other (the mind) so that true knowledge is possible. This would be constituted, for Descartes, by "evident" rather than "traditional" ideas. What is operative here is the conviction that reason is the instrument that readily apprehends reality. This is precisely rationalism, and its serious problem, according to Marías, is its contention that our idea *is* reality itself as viewed by us. This, of course, prevents us from looking at things. Idealism emerged from this, denying that things exist independently of ideas; and ultimately Kant denied that things can be viewed as they are "in themselves." Both positions created the problematic situation of which our time is heir. Thus, "today our problem is precisely the solution of Descartes."[7] We need to transcend traditional ideas to reach reality.

Before turning to a closer look at the problem of what philosophy has become in our day, we must examine what became of it during that period known as the Enlightenment, a period in which ration-

alism was spread rather thinly among a great number of "thinkers."
The "faith" in reason that had dominated modern philosophers was
held by only a few intellectual giants, keeping in touch through
correspondence. It came to dominate whole circles of people during
the period of the Enlightenment, developing into a part of the
societal circumstance. If anything, the eighteenth-century Enlightenment could not tolerate mystery, and was determined to use
philosophy to change the structure of society. The enlightened
minorities attempted to live directly from ideas and without even
social beliefs, which have always sustained men. They succeeded
only in *believing in* ideas. Reason attempted to impose its structure
on society without regard to the reality itself. An "optimism of
reason" set in that maintained that reality would behave as our
minds behave, yielding to our ideas and the desires behind them.
(The culmination of this was the idea of progress, a notion that
dominated Europe until World War I.) The reaction to this optimism was eventually to be irrationalism.

Putting aside a consideration of positivism in the nineteenth
century, as a continuation of rationalism in which there is an
attempt to convert philosophy into a scientific method, the most
striking feature of the irrationalism of the nineteenth century is its
discovery of human life as the subject of philosophical consideration.
In philosophy the nineteenth century began rather late, after the
crisis in German idealism around 1830. Nevertheless, the philosophy
of that century bore the influence of the thought of Hegel. Slowly,
against idealism that converts things into the "I" and positivism
that reduces the "I" to a thing, there came to emerge the insight
that the "I" is not a thing, that the substance of life is history, that
it is man himself who changes. Noting the shortcomings of "pure"
(mathematico-physical) reason as applied to life and history, Dilthey
posited a new form of reason that was broad enough to include
history. Yet, his historicism considered life's fundamental issues to
be beyond the scope of philosophy. It remained for Ortega, Marías
contends, to expand "historical reason" to become "vital" or
"living" reason, in which reason ". . . is life in its function of
enabling us to apprehend reality intellectually."[8] Philosophy as
meaning the use of "vital reason" to apprehend human life as the
fundamental reality is the result. This is Marías's position, following
Ortega, and Marías considers his mentor the most creative philosopher of the twentieth century.

We have seen that philosophy is understandable only to the

degree to which we are able to see it as part of the situation in which it originates. The changing meanings of philosophy are connected to changing needs felt by men in their various historical circumstances. If we take any one meaning, the rest seem to be excluded. This is because ". . . for each philosopher, philosophy is what he has himself created."[9] Philosophy is the philosopher's personal effort "to stay afloat," to reach radical certainty about those things that disturb him. Accordingly, there is a certain sameness among all philosophers insofar as philosophy is this human activity. Each realizes that in order to live in his circumstances he *must* philosophize.

III   *Philosophy as Responsible Vision*

On various occasions Marías has emphasized that, rather than having a method, philosophy *is* method. It is now necessary to ask: In what does philosophy as method consist? Following Ortega, Marías agrees that philosophy's only method is that of Jericho, that is, the making of repeated circles—ever more narrow—around things, approaching them until they reveal themselves, until the "walls" that hide them crumble, even as did those of Jericho, to expose their truth. Marías prefers to use the Greek term *alétheia* to make his point, attributing its first philosophical utilization in our time to Ortega in *Meditations on Quixote*. *Alétheia* means that which is not covered up or hidden, that which is patent, manifest, or unveiled. In contrast, the Latin term for truth, *veritas*, means exactness and strictness in utterance (retained in our word "veracity"), and the Hebrew term for truth, *emunah* (from the same root as *amen*), means truth in the sense of trustworthy (as when we say a "true" friend).

Even as falsehood is covering up, truth involves uncovering. It is primarily an unveiling or demonstrating of what things are. "The decisive point is that philosophical truth does not consist only in the moment of *alétheia*, of discovery or patentization and, in consequence, of a vision; at the same time it requires the seizure or possession of that seen reality."[10] This is why Marías proposed a "definition" of philosophy as *responsible vision*.[11] To philosophize is to be constantly awake in order to attempt to discover and justify the truth of things by tearing away the traditional social interpretations that veil things as they are. It is the need to do so and the responsibility of doing so. Since the philosopher voluntarily does not "fall asleep" to reality, accepting it as it is, philosophy *is* liberty, even as is life. What a philosopher does in accepting reality is to think and rethink "what is reality?"—philosophy's main question—so that it is evident or justified to him.

We must not forget the function of a definition, including that of philosophy. To define is to delimit, signal, or mark out the limits of the theme being talked about to bring it into view and keep it from escaping or losing its contours. Otherwise, we might not agree as to what is being investigated; there could be a discrepancy and confusion as to what is being talked about. But, a definition alone cannot tell us "the how" or method by which a reality is to be investigated. It is merely the point from which we set out to reach reality. "Reality has a structure, which is imposed upon *all* thought, if it gets close enough to reality not to let it escape and does not replace it with its own construction."[12] Accordingly, our philosophic theory will have a systematic character, not because we may wish it—as happened in German idealism—but because reality itself is systematic and this should determine theory. Philosophic truth is systematic in the sense that each affirmation in philosophy is effectively upheld by all the others. That is, strictly speaking, what makes them true, and this is why philosophy is content only with the whole truth. None of the statements would be true if removed from the context of the others. Even as any one of the elements or ingredients of reality implies the rest, so with the statements of philosophy.

If, in order to investigate reality, we start from Marías's definition of philosophy as responsible vision, what would we be doing? The traditional method of obtaining knowledge about reality has been by explanation, by taking apart the elemental components of that reality in order to reduce it to its simpler elements. Such an explanatory method is valid only if the reality being considered is reducible. It destroys, rather than preserves, that reality which is irreducible (as human life as fundamental or radical reality will be found to be). To turn to description as a method for such an irreducible reality is more accurate. However, description alone, even phenomenological description, gives us only unconnected notes or data. This is hardly sufficient for one to decide how to live, to orient himself in respect to the *total* situation in which he finds himself. "In order to live, it is necessary to go beyond description, to reach a meaning or a theory . . . which is required and imposed upon us by reality itself and by the vital necessity of deciding and choosing."[13] Thus, to live we must apprehend reality intrinsically, as it is in all its actual connections apart from our ideas. This is possible because "life is the concrete form of reason."[14] Life is possible for me only if I inquire after and discover a basis for its meaning or intelligibility in the actual structure of reality. In other words, living demands reason, and that reason—the apprehension of reality in all its actual and concrete connections—functions only in living. This is why the method of philosophy is vital reason, with its double signification of reason (meaning) as that without which life is impossible, and reason (the apprehension of the connectedness of reality) as that which life is. The inexorable mission of life is to give an account of itself. We feel we have to give a reason for everything we do.

What, may we ask, is the structure of the philosophic theory created by this method of vital reason? First we must see what theory is. "Theory means vision or contemplation. This means that it is the result of an action performed by someone; the elimination of the person who sees or understands, of the subject of that theory, is a surreptitious amputation of its true reality."[15] This, as we saw, is the reason philosophy can be said to have a biography. It is also why philosophic theory, being intrinsically dynamic in its flow, has a dramatic structure. As a necessary theory of human life in order to live authentically, philosophy is both a humble and a proud task. Its theories are essential and sober dramas needed for living.

Philosophic theory must justify itself in the sense of not relying on other theories and by "giving reasons for" all its truths, rather than accepting interpretations. Only in this sense is philosophy, especially metaphysics, without assumptions. Partial truths are insufficient because they preclude, and may even produce, a radical or fundamental uncertainty concerning what human life is—an uncertainty philosophy tries to overcome. At most, philosophy sets out from partial certainties and from them derives its stimuli and problems. It must justify all its presuppositions by analyzing them, by making them the object of investigation. In the end, philosophy justifies itself only when the situation in which a man finds himself is such that it leads him to philosophize or theorize about his life in order that he can live. As such, philosophy can be said to be a "sufficient knowledge of human life," sufficient to enable us to know what to hold onto and to live authentically. To show that this way of knowing must not be disengaged from its historical movement, Marías quotes Ortega's words: "The most truthful definition of philosophy that can be given . . . would be this one, of a chronological nature: philosophy is an occupation toward which Western man felt himself forced from the sixth century B.C. onward and which with surprising continuity he has kept pursuing until the present day."[16]

IV   *Philosophy as Metaphysics*

Since the periods of intense philosophical activity are those in which metaphysics is pursued while those in which philosophy wanes and is in crisis are those in which it is neglected, abandoned, or denied, our next step must be an examination of philosophy as metaphysics, as seen in Marías's essay on "The Idea of Metaphysics." After examining the origin of the word and recording some of the vicissitudes it has suffered, without attempting a complete history of the term, he put forth his own position, claiming for it "considerable innovation," even if it is traditional insofar as it tries to correspond to what the intention of metaphysics has been from the beginning. What this intention always has been is to be the science of the fundamental or radical reality, and in this sense it is identical with philosophy itself.

The word "metaphysics" as such is meaningless, being a transliteration from the Latin which, in turn, is itself a transliteration from four Greek words meaning "those [books] after the physics [books]." It just so happened that Andronicus of Rhodes, in the first century B.C., arranged the works of Aristotle such that certain of his writings, fourteen books in all, came to be placed after those on physics or nature. (Eventually this spatial designation, signifying lineal order, will designate levels of reality and "postphysics" will become "transphysics" or the "supernatural.") The content of those books, the first attempt to synthesize this kind of knowing, is designated by Aristotle himself with four principal terms: wisdom, first philosophy, knowledge gained by inquiry, and theory of truth. The first two terms are hierarchical designations, simply pointing to that kind of knowledge that is ultimate and supreme. The third term indicates that a method is needed to arrive at a result that was initially lacking. The fourth term, as Marías interprets it, is the main clue to what Aristotle was attempting and to what metaphysics should be. It means the same for Aristotle as "philosophizing about the truth" rather than, as earlier man had done, "theologizing about the truth." In theologizing the gods speak "truthfully" to man about reality, while in philosophizing man himself "uncovers" reality and it shows itself to him "in truth," that is, for what it is. With philosophy man no longer needs passively to rely on an oracle as an intermediary but actively addresses himself directly to reality and compels it to respond by using a method. Thus, metaphysics originates in man's effort to escape ignorance and seek wisdom on his own so as to be able to orient himself, not in regard to this or that particular thing, but to the *one* fundamental reality latent and hidden beneath the *many* things. Such is the origin of metaphysics and the task men set for it, a task attempted throughout the longest portion of its history, from Plato in the fourth century B.C. until the crisis that culminated in the eighteenth century with Kant, who questioned the very possibility of metaphysics.

In the intervening years the history of metaphysics was closely connected with Aristotle's original presentation of being and the modes of being. After having been lost, his work was rediscovered and gave the impetus in the Middle Ages to what can be called the culmination of metaphysics in Muslim, Jewish, and Christian Scholasticism. Despite the fact that a large portion of medieval work in metaphysics was a commentary on Aristotle, the changed historical situation of revealed religion, and the intention of philosophers to be theologians of that religion, gave quite a different orientation to the discipline. In their work metaphysics became combined with theology via their efforts to understand religious notions, especially that of creation in which existence is opposed to nothingnesss rather than, as the Greeks held, to nonexistence.

During the fourteenth century the union of the two distinguishable disciplines of metaphysics (philosophy) and theology (religion) was gradually coming to an end. The trend of disengagement culminated in metaphysics becoming independent and autonomous in the work of Suárez at the end of the sixteenth century. The result of the separation was that metaphysics became a solely speculative science, the contemplation—for its own sake—of the truth about being, rather than connected with the attainment of happiness as it had been among the Greeks and the medievals, for whom contemplation of the highest being was the highest form of living. In the work of Descartes, and those directly or indirectly influenced by him, the major problem in metaphysics became the communicability or interaction of the two fundamentally different kinds of substances or beings: thinking substances (God and minds) and extended substances (all things or bodies, including the human body).

By the time of Kant's critique of "pure" reason, metaphysics had been ridiculed by the Renaissance humanists for its abstract and sterile debates. The French Encyclopedists had criticized it for its mutually contradictory positions and the "transnatural" or "immaterial" character of its objects of study; and the empiricists, especially Hume, had reproached it for its inability to prove through experience the existence of substance, soul, causality, and God. Kant's conclusion was that metaphysics as a speculative discipline, in which the philosopher acquired genuine knowledge about the world, the soul, and God, was impossible, since such knowledge would have to be based on sensation, which does not present us with the "thing-in-itself," that is, reality as it really is, but only the "thing-as-it-appears" in sensation. What was left was merely metaphysics as a natural tendency to go beyond the given in experience, yielding ideas that are regulative for grouping our experiences. The realities supposedly proved by traditional metaphysics are, at most, postulates of "practical" reason of use solely in morality.

Kant's conclusion was accepted, to varying degrees, by the predominant philosophies of the nineteenth century. Metaphysics grew to be so despised and forbidden that a doctrine or line of reasoning could be disqualified by simply being labeled "metaphysical" (and, in some circles, still is). On the one hand, there were positivists who did metaphysics in spite of themselves, with an antimetaphysical metaphysics, and on the other hand, those who continued to engage in the discipline as if Kant had never lived. In between were the few whose work, always with Kant in mind, eventually led to the present day "return to metaphysics," despite the lingering of the antimetaphysical attitudes in the "scientific," analytic, and linguistic forms of contemporary philosophy—for all of which, in varying degrees, metaphysical statements simply make no sense, that is, are meaningless.

The virtual disappearance of metaphysics in the eighteenth and nineteenth centuries was due, in large part, to the change in the direction of attention and interest of philosophers. From an earlier primary concern with the problem of God, immortality, and theology there was a shift to the problems of the origin of ideas, knowledge, and the natural sciences. Only those interested in traditional problems, mainly Catholic theologians, kept alive an interest in metaphysics. Three motives led to the eventual restoration of the discipline. First was the desire, motivated by theological concerns, to vindicate and justify metaphysics against modern philosophy (as with the Neo-Scholastics). Second was the desire to regain objectivity in knowing against subjectivism (as with Husserl).

Third was the discovery of certain realities, or aspects of reality, that are radical or fundamental (as with Ortega, who maintained that this was the case with "my life"). Thus, for Marías, following Ortega, ". . . the theory of human life, understood, as theory, is not the propaedeutics of metaphysics, is not its preparation, but is metaphysics." [17]

CHAPTER 3

Human Life and Its Characteristics

I *Metaphysics as Theory of Human Life*

TO ANSWER philosophy's main question, "What is man," we must begin by turning to the study of fundamental reality, which is metaphysics. (The other, inseparable, question of philosophy, "What is to become of me," will be considered at the end of this chapter.) This radical reality, in the sense of being the root of all other realities and itself irreducible to any other, is "my life." We can avoid giving this expression unjustifiable biological overtones by adhering, as Ortega once proposed, to the meaning "my life" has when we spontaneously use it in ordinary, rather than scientific, discourse. That is, it is to be understood in the biographical sense, irreducible to the biological but unintelligible without it.

If each of us looks into his respective "my life," we see that it is the stage upon which all of our experiences show themselves, the arena in which each of us comes in contact with all kinds of realities. In "my life" I find things and myself, myself with things, doing something with things—what Ortega meant by saying "I am I [myself] and my circumstances" in *Meditations on Quixote*. "My life" is the reality prior to these other realities. It is what remains when I eliminate all other realities that appear as grounded or rooted in it, including my "I" and all other possible forms of life, from the vegetative and animal to the extraterrestrial, angelic, and divine. It is likewise what remains when I remove all my ideas, theories, or interpretatations.

The philosophic study of "my life" ". . . is the search for radical certitude concerning radical reality."[1] If this definition is not to become a colossal triviality, it must be taken in its strictest sense, paying special attention to the use of the adjective "radical" to modify "certitude" and "reality," for ". . . on the precise meaning of this adjective depends this [Marías's] whole idea of

56

metaphysics."[2] Above all, it depends on how it modifies "certitude." Knowledge that is certain is not just any information, regardless of how true it may be, but only that which I need to know in order to live. The absence of truth as simple exactitude never calls into question "my life" and how I ought to live it. Radical certitude is truth about how I must live, a truth at which I arrive because I find it imperative to know, for otherwise I could not live.

It is from "my life" that I form the theory of human life, upon finding other realities that also function as "I's" and realizing the disjunctive character of life (life as this one *or* that one). The relation of "my life" to "life" is not that of an individual to its species such that the common notes shared by *all* individuals would be sufficient to understand *any* individual, as it is with things. Each life is conditioned by shared living, is a "this one" rather than a "that one," so that it has no meaning without bringing in other lives. Human life is not the usual type of universal, since it is unintelligible without circumstantializing it, without bringing in other human lives. Thus, the intrinsic necessity of knowing "my life" leads to the intrinsic necessity of knowing "human life," and is the ultimate justification for metaphysics, the minimal theory needed to live.

The method that is metaphysics cannot be explanation, the traditional form of knowledge obtained by taking apart or analyzing the elemental components of a thing such that it is reduced to another thing or many things. That which is unexchangeable, irreplaceable, and irreducible, such as "my life," would be destroyed by this method, and the irrationalism of recent times is correct in rejecting it. Description is an improvement, but it is not enough. Besides describing "my life" I must form projects, ultimately choosing one, in respect to the facilities and difficulties with which I am confronted in order to function in the entire vocation or program that constitutes myself. What description uncovers is reality in all its connections, the real unity in which each reality is constituted, by being co-implicated in all others. Without such an apprehension "my living" is impossible, resulting in mere activity rather than human performance. Without an essential and prior pause (*detención*) by which I orient myself to my circumstances, discovering the actual interconnectedness of things, "my living" would not be "mine." Human living is possible only if I use my reason to discover the implications of one reality for another, thereby giving meaning to "my living." To the co-implication of reason and life Marías, following Ortega, gives the name "vital reason" (*razón vital*), signifying that life without reason is impossible and that reason is what life is, in the sense that reason functions in apprehending reality in its connections. Thus, the method that is metaphysics can be no other than vital reason, and in this sense metaphysics is intrinsically necessary in order to live humanly. The only way of cognitively apprehending reality by this method is narration, by relating what is going on in "my living."

Of course, I can only narrate some "thing." That is, I can understand "my life" only in reference to the structure of human life. This structure can be discovered only by an analysis of individual life, primarily mine, since human life does not exist except in the concretion of "my life." Marías accepts Ortega's definition of structure—as given in *Meditations on Quixote*—as elements *plus* order. Structure is the organizing or interpreting that we do with the "raw" elements we find in the experience of realities. It is not added to the ingredients of experience but is the connectedness of the elements, discovered by reason. In this sense and strictly speaking, we should not refer to the structure *of* reality but to reality *as* structure.

By a descriptive or phenomenological analysis of "my life" I discover certain structures, conditions, or requisites without which it, or any other human life, is not possible, what Marías refers to as the analytic structure of human life. These notes may be said to be four, each co-implied in the other, and still others implied in them. By using the method of Jericho we can say that each trait is a view of life from a certain distance or perspective. As we draw closer, in an ever-narrowing spiral, to the object of our philosophical conquest, we see ever more clearly or truthfully what we had seen less clearly from the previous position. As we draw closer we realize that our newer sight was included or implied in the older one. The new view may seem like a repetition, but due to the spiral nature of our repeated cognitive circles, it is not quite the same. Even as life is not given all at once, so it is with knowledge.

The four notes may be said to be: personality, dynamism, necessity, and circumstantiality, their maximum condensation being Ortega's thesis that "I am I and my circumstances." A brief explication of the thesis shows that the first "I" is the I as a "who," as a project or vital program and, so, not a thing. Such is what is meant by personality, and it is the first view we receive in analyzing our lives. As we move closer we see that life is a doing, a thing to be done or a project to be realized—what is meant by dynamism. Life is not quiescent but an activity that *needs* to be done, I choosing to do something with things, precisely what is entailed by necessity. These things, including other people, surround or circumscribe me, offering a repertory of possibilities and impossibilities, acting as a stage in or on which I act out my life. This is what the requisite of circumstantiality involves. These universal structures are fleshed out, so to speak, by the concrete elements found in individual biographies, throwing greater light on the implications of the four main traits.

Life as a thing necessarily to be done indicates its essentially historical nature. Human life happens; it has a temporal and successive quality that reveals life's finitude and mortality. Life's temporality is indicated in memory, which retains selected portions of the past, and in imagination, which anticipates certain aspects of the future. Knowledge is conditioned by temporality, as is volition. Thus, we are constitutively insecure, ignorant, perplexed, and dissatisfied, traits which will be examined further in later sections of this chapter, especially when happiness as part of philosophy's second main question, "What will become of man?," is treated. Circumstantiality, the last trait we notice in our cognitive apprehension of our lives, is especially rich in implications. That there is something besides myself in "my life," corporeal things in a world, implies not only that I am "in" the world and in some sense corporeal, but also that my living is a living-with. Once we discover that certain of those things are other "I's," this essential trait of living-with can be termed our sociality. That is, human life is constitutively social. In order to be *in* "my life" and *with* my world I must be installed in that world, an installation, as we shall see, that is as dynamic as is human living itself.

Let us examine in more detail the most fundamental of these essential traits. Life as personality raises the theme of the person, one of the most difficult and elusive in the entire history of philosophy. Around it have occurred some of the most important changes in that history. What comes to mind is the philosophical consideration by the medieval Scholastics of the person in the context of the Christian belief in the Trinity, and the identification of person with mind which Descartes, at the beginning of modern philosophy, characterized as consciousness. These attempts fell short of an adequate understanding of the person precisely because they utilized categories, or ways of thinking, more appropriate to things. The Greek notion of substance, adopted by Boethius in the sixth

century A.D. in his famous definition of person and passed on to the
later Scholastics, as well as the Cartesian notion of *res* (Latin for
"thing"), are both applicable precisely to things. For Marías,
following the position of Ortega, the person is *not* a thing. Things,
above all, are fully real; they are "there" and "given." As we saw in
presenting the biography of philosophy as a human endeavor, a
human being as person is precisely that reality "who" is partially
unreal, "who" is not all "there" but "is arriving." Stated differently,
a person is not only real or present but also unreal insofar as he is
turned toward the future as a project or program to be realized. A
person already is, of course, but his present being is "to be arriving."
Every strictly human relationship, above all friendship and love,
indicates this, for it reveals that being real is "to keep on being," a
condition of constantly arriving and setting forth. This unique
condition of human reality is why the main question of philosophy
should be "*Who* am I?" rather than "*What* is man?," for "what-
ness" has a connotation of being a static, given thing.

II   *Empirical Structure of Human Life: "Man"*

The question at this point, as Marías sees it, is: Can we pass
directly from the analytical structure to the individual, circumstantial, and concrete reality in understanding the biography of an
individual human being? His answer: No. There is a missing stratum
of reality and a level of theory between them, of which he became
suspicious when comparing the dictionary entries of three very
different realities: pentagon, owl, and Cervantes. The dictionary
gives a *definition* of pentagon, an ideal object, by giving its essence.
Of the owl, a real object, a *description* is presented by saying what
it looks like and how it behaves. Concerning Cervantes, a story, a
biographical *narration*, is offered that includes where and when he
was born, where he traveled and lived, whom he married, what he
did and wrote, and where he died. The biography of Cervantes
clearly presupposes the analytical or general theory of human life,
but there is another series of assumptions implied, those which
Marías will call collectively "man." For example, the entry says
Cervantes's arm was left maimed as a result of a war wound, but the
analytical theory says nothing about arms, indicating that having
arms is not an ingredient of human life in general.[3] Likewise with
regard to his marriage and death as an old man, for the general
theory makes no reference to sex and marriage or to ages and
growing old. To this intermediate area, with which Marías had been

concerned for over a quarter of a century, he eventually gave the name of empirical structure. All those determinations belong to it that—without being part of the analytical structure—are not chance, coincidental, or factual; like the analytical structure it is previous to each concrete biography.

As might be expected, Marías acknowledges, classical philosophy did not find the theme completely alien. Aristotle, in positing the distinction between the being that is *per se* (essential or substantial) and *per accidens* (nonessential or accidental), did discover that there is something more, something between the other two. Characteristics such as "man's" being a biped, having the quality of laughter, and being subject to the greying of his hair are neither essential nor simply accidental. Without being essential they coincide with the limits of the species "man." That is, all "men," and only "men," have these "properties." Porphyry adopted the idea and the Scholastics, receiving it from both these philosophers, incorporated it into their various systems. Marías's theory, he maintains, differs basically from all of theirs. The properties of which they spoke were notes of a substance in reference to things, while in Marías's position it is not a question of things but of life as a dramatic reality taking place, a reality that exhibits a structure.

The characteristics that actually comprise the empirical structure are not necessary for each and every possible human life, but belong only in fact to all those human lives we empirically encounter in this world. Human life must have one empirical structure or another, making it an ingredient of the analytical structure as implied in circumstantiality, especially but not precisely the one that it does have in this world. Marías maintains that human life can be conceived of in other worlds, with other forms of corporeity, sense powers, and life spans. Indeed, this is why—Marías is convinced—"man" will be disappointed if he does not encounter human or biographical and personal life with a different empirical structure when he arrives on other planets.

To examine only the components of "man's" empirical structure would yield what Marías consider to be the science of anthropology. To ground or root these characteristics in the traits of the analytical structure results in a task proper to philosophy, what he calls metaphysical anthropology. As a result, it will be seen that "man" is the animal who has a human life, the articulation of a "who" (the "I") with a "what" (my circumstances, including my body).[4] These various components exist in a manner best described as being vectorially installed. The use of the vector, with its symbol of the arrow, indicates the dynamic, future-oriented nature of every vital action, permitting the intellection not only of biographical life but of the complexly balanced system of material structures of biographical life upon which it is based.

The dynamic and dramatic reality of human living is difficult to understand because the usual linguistic form we use to speak of it acts as an obstacle. The verb "to be" (*ser*), when used to designate life is, at most, a secondary verb useful for understanding derived determinations of the primary reality which is "to live."[5] This is true of the verb in the various languages of the greatest philosophical traditions in the West: Greek, Latin, French, English, and German. But, in Spanish, of which little use has been made in philosophy until recently—since the earlier Spaniards wrote in Latin—there are two forms of the verb "to be": *ser* and *estar*. *Ser* is used to designate inherentness and permanency, while *estar* refers to mere states or passing conditions and nonradical feelings. Marías, however, maintains that *estar*, necessarily referring to reality rather than merely to fiction, can also indicate the dynamic and at the same time stable reality of living. Moreover, *estar* indicates the essential circumstantiality of life, with the Latin root of *stare* imbedded in both *estar* and "circumstance." The full impact of this is realized when we say "I am living" (*estoy viviendo*), using the true gerundive rather than the present participle, and implying that I am not a thing among the things that stand around me, but that I am doing something with things to make "my life."

In the "doing" that is living there is a "coming from" the past and a "going toward" the future, revealing the "arriving" quality of living. Because language is designed primarily to name static and fixed things, we must constantly resort to the use of metaphors and figures of speech to enable us to look in the direction where we discover the reality of living. Thus, human life can be compared to an arrow advancing in a forward direction. Strictly speaking, it is the entire bow and arrow that is more adequate as the symbol of life, the bow with its background tension (my past) from which the arrow (my specific projects) receives its impulse and its target toward which it is aimed (my future). In human life the target, to be one, must be sought or chosen by the arrow, usually out of several possible targets. Furthermore, human life as a "to-be-living" is not a mere succession of events, one target after another, but a process of continuous aiming and firing that indicates a simultaneous structural and shifting character.

Our installation is multiple or, if you wish, our unitary vital installation is in various dimensions. The different forms of installation of human life are never definitively listed by Marías, although he speaks of three being so general that they become confused, unless we are careful, with the human condition itself: worldhood, sensibility, and corporeality. The forms he lists are those that have become relevant under certain conditions. The implication is that there are still others, including those that have ceased to be relevant to such an extent that they do not even seem real to us. Those that are listed are: (1) *sexuate condition,* or the fact that human life on earth occurs in a disjunctive form of man *or* woman (to be examined in the following section of this chapter); (2) *age,* or the successive stages from which I make my life (to be seen in the fourth section of this chapter); (3) *race,* in the sense of "historicized biology," that gives a repertory of modes of living; (4) *caste,* different from race, because it always functions along with other castes in giving a repertory of actions; (5) *social class,* which also gives a repertory of activity; and (6) *language,* which determines the structure of the world as a sum of realities in certain precise connections, besides conferring a given tone upon it,[6] because temper (*temple*) is a modulation of all forms of installation. For example, a priest or nun is not installed sexually in the same mode as a married man or woman, an "Uncle Tom" is installed differently in his race than is a Black Panther, and I speak differently when I am angry than when I am happy.

To be "in" a world, one world or another, as a boundary for my projects and a means through which other forms of installation are possible, is implied in circumstantiality. Marías designates this world as "worldhood," and calls the actual manner of "man's" being "in" and "with" his world sensibility or transparency, since I am with things "through" my body. The various senses of which sensibility is composed enable me to discover various aspects of the world, introducing a "plot" into the world itself, because we fill in with our imagination that sense data which we do not receive from that which we do. Thus, worldhood and corporeality are inseparably linked, for corporeality is the concrete form in which I am installed in this world. I am in the world in a bodily *manner,* not as a thing among things, projectively installed in my body. I am (*estoy*) corporeally.

In a certain sense, linguistic installation envelops the others, for language is the first or primary form of interpretation of reality since we express the other forms linguistically. Philosophy as an *explicitly* rational interpretation of reality, possible only when realized linguistically, takes its point of departure from linguistic interpretation.[7] Philosophy's degree of authenticity in answering its basic question, "What type of reality does this or that have?," depends to a great extent on a given language's possibilities (as we saw earlier when Marías examined the Spanish forms of the verb "to be").

In developing his position on linguistic installation, Marías is following Ortega's "great discovery," as he calls it, namely, the grounding of language in the more radical phenomenon of saying or utterance. Utterance is a requisite for all human life, for "my life" would be impossible without my uttering to others and to myself. The intrinsic theory of human life discussed earlier, by which I acquire the necessary knowledge of myself and my circumstances in order to go on living, bears witness to this. The form of utterance that "man" has, in fact, is speech or language, which is possible only because he has a certain empirical structure. "Man" is aerial rather than aquatic, making his auditory system more developed, and has special vocal organs arranged around that muscle called the tongue. Language in the concrete is in the form of languages or tongues, each proper to a given historico-social reality whose members feel their idiom as intimately theirs. They live, move, and are in their language, speaking Greek*ly* for example.[8]

III   *Sexuate Installation and Love*

The linguistic distinction in Spanish between the two adjectives *sexual* ("sexual") and *sexuado* ("sexuate") is employed by Marías in discussing sex as a form of installation, a distinction he finds exceedingly useful. Sexual activity is a small and limited, even if very important, province of our life, not beginning at birth and usually ending before death. It is founded on something more basic, the sexuate condition of human life on earth, a condition affecting all of life at all times and in all its dimensions.

A moment's reflection is sufficient to make us realize that what is called "man" does not exist. Human life appears in this world in two profoundly different forms: men and women. The use of the word "man" to designate both is common in many languages, even if carelessly inaccurate. (Marías, nevertheless, chose to retain it, putting the word in quotes when it refers to both men and women, as we have done in this chapter.) The different forms do not constitute two classes of one species *Homo,* for this would be contrary to all biological usage. On the other hand, the sexuate condition cannot be considered accidental in the sense in which it is so to be blond or brunette, tall or short. The sexuate condition belongs neither to the analytical structure nor to the accidental, but to that intermediate structure called empirical.

The sexuate installation is a disjunctive one, with "man" being male *or* female. Disjunction must not be confused with division. Balls of two different colors, for example, can be divided into different piles, a division that also separates and makes each independent of the other. Disjunction, on the contrary, links; it is present in both terms of the disjunction. Each sex affects the other by co-implicating, or "complicating," the other in a relationship of polarity. Being installed in our sex vectorily, we project ourselves toward the opposite sex, indicating that *each* sexuate condition is intrinsically insufficient. This makes plural human life a dynamic living-with, for the sexuate installation introduces an active configuration resembling a magnetic field, even previous to all sexual behavior. Indeed, *all* behavior, sexual and asexual, is unintelligible without this prior installation that pervades, permeates, and encompasses all of life. "All of reality, even that most remote from sexuality—eating, comprehension of a mathematical theorem, contemplation of a landscape, a religious action, the experience of danger—is lived out of installation in [one's] sex, and therefore within a context, and from a perspective that cannot be reduced to the other [sex]."[9]

As an installation, sex is not only a biological fact but a psychic and historico-social one as well. This is obvious from the reaction to a newborn baby. The words "it's a boy" or "it's a girl" mean more than biological identification. They set in motion a number of other factors that interpret the biological, however much distinctions are becoming less rigorous: the colors and kinds of clothing, the types of games, plans for the future, etc. Abnormalities in the biological can affect the biographical sexuate condition, but this depends on a number of factors: their concrete content, the date at which they occur, how they are experienced by the individual, and their social interpretation. However, even without biological abnormalities there can be biographical ones.

The part of the body through which one's sexuate condition is most manifest in the biological sense is, of course, the genitals. But, it is through the face, only minimally sexual or erogenous, that one's sexuate condition in the biographical sense is most evident and which is most erotic. In a very real sense the countenance functions as the abbreviated representative of the whole body and person, alluding to them as a repertory of possibilities. A person is maximally living in his face, and those who can read the alphabet proper to it and its historico-social circumstance learn the truest knowledge of a person.

When we look into the faces of a man and a woman, what does each express? According to Marías, the face of a man reveals him as successful or not, just as that of a woman shows her as beautiful or not. This is Marías's initial response, and by the time he has considered the virile and feminine "figures" more closely his conclusion is: man's face shows his "strength" and woman's her "grace." In speaking of the male Marías opts for the old Spanish word *gravedad*. Man must recognize and accept the burden of life that comes with being a male, bearing and enduring it even if he manages to cover it up with joviality, high spirits, or humor. "With his grave face man looks at woman, looks at the beautiful face of the woman for whom it has been worthwhile to endure gallantly the burden of life."[10] The beauty that is characteristic of the feminine face is that which expands toward the future so that we feel that we can go on looking at it all our lives. It is a grace that is winged, light, as opposed to the gravity of the male. Woman's mission is to draw upward, herself and the man attracted to her, to lead man and capture him with her intimacy and invite him to settle down in an inwardness.

These anthropological statements must be understood in their proper metaphysical context. From the general traits of the analytical theory of human life we see implied the basic, constitutive insecurity of human life. Life consists in the necessity of having to do something with its circumstances, a task that must be accomplished despite "man's" ignorance, indecision, and helplessness. The male knows this, yet—with respect to woman—he is characterized by the exact opposite. He must attempt to have strength or valor, or he feels a lack and believes himself inferior to his condition. This strength is not confined, of course, to mere physical power or sexual potency, although it may have been in earlier times. What is important is man's *pretension* to be exactly the opposite of what human life constitutively is. It is not a matter of feigning what "man" is not, but of putting forth the effort to create an island of security that he carries on his shoulders as culture, that includes philosophy, science, technology, the state, etc. The female, on the other hand, knows she must be beautiful, with a beauty of the interior person that illuminates her physical features. If she does not try to be such, she does not function as a woman but has betrayed her condition.[11] (This is not to deny that the male also has beauty, even if in him it is not his primary quality, or that the female has strength and valor.)

The male's offer of strength to the female must not be misinterpreted as meaning he offers her protection, which would be paternalism and eventually reduce her to a minor. Any man who needs to regard a woman as inferior is precisely one who does not feel sure of his masculine condition. Indeed, protection is more an ingredient of the feminine condition, exercised with respect to her children and, secondarily, her husband. At most, man offers woman his strength and she "resorts" to it. To speak of equality between man and woman ". . . is one of the most dangerous stupidities into which one could possibly fall."[12] Instead of equality there can, and should, be an equilibrium between the sexes, a dynamic balance, constituted by inequality and tension, that keeps man and woman on the same level. In this balance is to be found the male's "overlordship" (*senorío*) ruled by his "enthusiasm" for woman, as a result of which everything he does he does *for* woman. The correlative of this overlordship is "surrender," woman freely stepping into the shelter offered by man. "She is supported by masculine gravity, and then is able to fulfill her problematic destiny of being a creature without gravity. The polarity of the sexuate condition rests on this: man does not want to protect woman, envelop her, shelter her . . . ; what he truly wants is suspend her in the air, to carry her upward."[13]

The most complete form of relationship between man and woman is the amorous condition, in which all the previous forms of installation converge. This condition rests on the underlying metaphysical trait of the neediness of human life. Since I am I and my circumstances, I need other human lives to become myself. The need I have for another person is not like that for things. I can always answer that I need things, including the talents or characteristics of certain people, by saying "because." Only a significant portion of my biography, or all of it, can answer why I need a person, for I need another person in order to become myself. Since human life is given in this world in a disjunctive fashion, the basic need—more than just biological—is of one sex for the other, a heterosexuate need. Of course, each sex also needs others of the same sexuate condition, although it is not the basic need. There is no undifferentiated need of simply one person for another, according to Marías.[14] Likewise, there is no general and undifferentiated love which is applicable to all relationships, for love in the strict sense is that between man and woman, woman and man, with all other biographical forms of love, including the love of God, derived from it.[15]

Like every installation, a person is installed in love, carrying out all his specific acts of love from it. Unlike all others, this form is strictly individual and personal rather than collective in nature. Too much attention has been given to the process of *falling in* love with a neglect of *being in* love. Being in love is being installed with a certain woman toward whom I project myself vectorially. I am in love when, after falling in love, I find that I am a different person, he who cannot become himself without the other person. I feel that before I was not truly the person I had to be; any previous love affairs are not worth talking about. My present love projects itself over my past life, reconstructing it so that it seems a preparation for this love. Even if I had not always been in love with this person, the "I" who now loves does so out of the reality I always was. I also feel that I will always be in love with this same person, for I cannot conceive of myself as being myself without loving this person. When I no longer feel this way, I am no longer in love. Such real love can outlast the death of one of the lovers, for the deceased continues as an essential part of the reality of the still-living person, even if in the form of a privation.[16]

There are those who fear being in love and resort to physical love, and even to affection, tenderness, and attachment, to avoid love in the strict sense. Physical love is the desire of another's body rather than loving *bodily*. Even if the other's body may be an initial attraction, being in love means that I love the other's body precisely because it is hers. This again shows that love is not strictly biological. It has a "story line," is a happening, has a history, is dramatic with a plotlike reality. Love's permanence, unless it is merely sexual, is the same as that of life itself, an arriving with another person toward the selves each feel he/she must become—must become together. Such a lasting love is built on the foundation of intersexual friendship, the best sort of friendship, a rare occurrence in past ages but a definite possibility in our century.[17]

IV   *Mortality: What is to become of me?*

Perhaps for the first time in history, twentieth-century thought has seriously considered temporality as a condition of human life. This points out that life in this world is not everlasting, beginning as it does at birth and ending at death, with its days numbered, whatever its "ulterior" fate may be. Life is possessed bit by bit, its mode of being is "to keep on being," or expressed more succintly, "to endure." What happens to us remains with us, gradually constituting the content of our lives. This past becomes the reality in my circumstances which the "executive I" must count upon when projecting me toward the future.

Temporality, which reveals itself to analysis as part of the necessary and universal structure of all human life, is conditioned by the various forms of the empirical structure in this world. For example, the temporal continuity of "man's" biography is modified by this world's structure of day and night, seasons and years, giving rise to age. Our lives are lived with time in mind, not the mere quantification of life's duration, but the time one can count on according to the current longevity. According to his age, which can be said to be "not yet," "now," or "no longer," "man" feels that he has accumulated so much experience and that life still holds out certain possibilities. The key factor about the last age of "man," old age, is that one cannot go beyond it. Being the last age, the old "man" must persevere in his vital phase, and this transforms the plotlike meaning of his life, so that the meaning of old age depends on how one confronts death, which is a "question mark."

Each age is lived in view of chance as an ingredient in our empirical structure. To live is, of course, to choose at every moment from the possibilities in my circumstances, including my past. But we choose in view of chance as the fortuitous and the unforeseeable. That a person teaches is a matter of choice; that he happens to have a certain student—as Ortega happened to have Marías—is a matter of chance. As we project forward we constantly modify our projects in view of chance happenings, just as a chess player does in view of his opponent's moves. The freedom involved in reacting to chance is inseparable from imagination, the seeing of the possibilities that confront us. The only thing that would be immune to chance would be precisely the one completely subject to necessity. Since life is not completely a thing, its combination of chance and necessity is what for thousands of years has been called destiny. Destiny is personal because it has to be adopted, accepted, appropriated, made mine. In this manner it becomes a vocation.

To the degree to which we realize our vocations and their aspirations, we can say we are happy, getting "a whiff of eternity." When I am happy, I feel that I am "in" the element of happiness, even though happiness is by definition a fleeting and faulty installation because of the constituent restlessness of life. If we succumb to the temptation to substitute the conditions of this world for those of a paradise, happiness will elude us, even in the form in which modern "man" in the West has settled for it: "for the moment everything is going well." The formula for happiness in loving a person is to include him or her in the texture of "my life," metaphorically pouring out ourselves to envelop each other, including each other in our vital projects. Happiness consists in the free and unconditional giving of myself while indifferent to any secondary grief. It is both a necessity, as the very reality of life, and an impossibility, for the intrinsic structural reason that life ends in death. Human life consists in trying to attain this "necessary impossibility," even as it consists of my attempt to attain myself.

This has brought us to the second question of the two that are the radical and inseparable ones that constitute philosophy: "What is to become of me?" If the answer to it is "nothing," if I die altogether, then nothing really matters, and one can be happy only to the degree to which death can be provisionally forgotten.[18]

Mortality has been used, for thousands of years, synonomously with "man." It means more than the fact that "man" *can* die, something extrinsic; it refers to the fact that "man" *must* die because of something intrinsic. Death, even if it turns out to be merely the end of biological life, must be lodged in "man's" biography, and all his choices must be made with this realization. We must resist the temptation to reduce "man's" death to the biological, even if it is easy to explain death in this manner. Death as biographical reveals the "unbridgeable ontological abyss" that separates "men" and animals, regardless of their biological continuity. Death is not a matter of abandoning corporeality, as the snake sheds its skin, and escaping intact toward another world. The point is that I die, and if the soul is mine, it too must experience death, even though it might not necessarily die.

Marías believes that both the position that man dies entirely and that only his body dies are phenomenologically unacceptable, unfaithful to reality as it is encountered. " 'Man,' the empirical structure of human life, is a closed structure; but *my life*, that is, I as person, is an open structure."[19] "What" I am is mortal; "who" I am consists in aspiring with an incessant hope to be immortal. To live is to anticipate and project into the future. I am so future oriented, so inexorably given over to futurizing, that there is no intrinsic reason why the plotlike projection of "my life" should be exhausted when I reach old age in this world. I cannot imagine myself as not being. I try to understand my own death by analogies, by creations of my imagination that link philosophy and literature (as in the works of Unamuno). Death is only intelligible to me when it is the death of another. The death of another, even of a loved one, is like an irrevocable and irreversible absence of the person; I continue to love the person, to be linked to my beloved, but in a different way.

The above is not offered by Marías as a "proof" for the immortality of the human person, even if we could agree on what constitutes proof in the case of human realities. Since we can imagine human life as having other forms,

[we] are able to imagine this life as the choice of the other life, the other as the realization of this. . . . It would be possible to think that reality in the other life [after death] would be determined by the authenticity and plenitude with which it has been desired or wished for in this life.

If this is so, we cannot know whether happiness is or is not a deceit. We have to live in insecurity, and any attempt to eliminate it, in one sense or another, is *either an act of* [philosophic or scientific] *intellectual disloyalty or an act of* [religious] *faith*. And then we must ask ourselves: what things are truly important in this life? For me, the norm is clear: those in respect to which death is not an objection, those to which I can radically say "yes"; those with which I project myself, because I desire them and want them forever, since without them I can not be truly "I."[20]

Now the reciprocal "exclusion" of the two fundamental and inseparable questions of philosophy can be seen: "Who am I?" and "What is to become of me?" According to Marías, the very dramatic character of human life consists in that exclusion. If I answer the first question by saying that I am "man," the answer to the second question must be nothing—not only does "man" die but I die. If I cannot answer the second question conclusively, as Marías says it cannot be, then death remains a question mark and I must live without knowing fully who I am, although living is the necessity of trying to know who I am. In this sense philosophy as well as happiness could be defined as a "necessary impossibility," although Marías himself does not make the connection.

CHAPTER 4

History and Society

I Co-living and Historicity: Traits of Human Life

I F WE imagine a given society at a specific moment in time, we find, first of all, a people collectively living in a certain place. Among those persons there exist relationships of different kinds, most of which do not belong to society in the strict sense, even if they are conditioned by the social modes in which they exist. All human relationships stem, of course, from human life and its essential or analytical structure. Circumstantiality as one of these essential features implies being installed in a world of things with which I coexist and of other people with whom I co-live.

Co-living is not something added to "my life," but is as much a constituent of it as are the other primary modes. Even when I am alone, I am in that mode of co-living that is called absence, for "my life" is circumstantial. This means that individual men do not exist in the plural but separately, deciding afterward to come together and live with each other in view of some purpose. Co-living, Marías insists, is in no way derivative and reducible as to a consequence of prior individual living.

It would be a mistake, however, to consider all co-living social in the strict sense, as has been the case with such greats in sociology as Emile Durkheim, Georg Simmel, and Max Weber. As early as the academic year 1934–1935, as a result of Ortega's seminar on "The Structure of Historical and Social Life," Marías became convinced that the distinction his mentor made between two different forms of co-living was absolutely essential in order to understand society, a distinction that Ortega ultimately called interindividual and social.[1] Co-living as interindividual is the living-with of individuals as such, of the individual who I am with the individual who you are, even if there are several individuals involved.[2] These relationships are constituted in the life of each of the individuals involved, for each

72

executes his act in view of some purpose directed toward a specific individual. Since each knows why he is acting and toward whom he is directing his activity, such interindividual acts are meaningful, as when my friend takes me by the arm at a gathering to inform me of our need to consult about a matter of mutual interest.

This act is quite different than that of wearing the outer clothing that I usually do. As a male I dress in a pair of pants and a jacket. Why? Did I invent this costume for myself? Did I choose it, after seeing others wear it, perhaps because I liked it or found it comfortable? No, to all these questions. It is not that I personally favor this dress as my usual accoutrement; it is that which one wears in my society because others wear it. I may even find the lapels on my jacket a costly waste of textile and absurd, and may even get my male friends to admit it, but we go on wearing it rather than a toga, doublet, or a frock coat. What is even more absurd, the choice of colors may be few, dark and somber, certainly not necessarily my favorite. If I choose a light blue—remember Marías is writing in the Spain of 1947—as a gentleman of the eighteenth-century French court or a fifteenth-century Florentine might have done, the reaction I might provoke would be, at the very mildest, ostracism—all because it is not the custom for one to dress as such in my day and age. When I attempt to trace this custom to its source in other people, I find it is nobody in particular, anybody, everybody—at least everybody who believes in the custom. These other people make their appearance in "my life" in a manner quite distinct from that of my parents, my brothers and sisters, my friends and acquaintances.[3] The "others" are impersonal, strictly speaking "nobody," and not the subject of an individual life who acts purposefully, meaningfully, and responsibly.

The social facts entailed in these social relationships are beliefs or customs, usages or binding observances (*vigencias*).[4] These facts are not things in the strict sense, since they are not part of nature, but realities created by humans. I cannot forget that they are real since I have to reckon with them; if I do not live by them, others retaliate. It makes no difference whether or not customs have a meaning, make sense in the light of my aspirations. They are imposed on all individuals, not on any one individual in particular, or on all classes, on what we call people. They function as pure, and often brutal, mechanisms that are unintelligible, irrational, and, therefore, literally dehumanizing. Yet they can—and do—have a beneficial effect, since customs are models of behavior that enable us to foresee the conduct of other individuals, especially strangers. Also, they oblige us to accept a certain heritage accumulated in the past, as well as to live at the level of the times. Finally, because they render a large part of our conduct automatic, customs free us to concentrate on more personal, creative, and truly human aspects of life, to form a more perfect future than we might otherwise have time to do.

If we return to our examination of a given society at a certain moment in time, we also discover data subject to statistics. The society has a definite number of inhabitants, constituted in a given number of families and grouped in certain ways (classes, etc.) to carry on a given quantity of professional activities that yield a certain amount of wealth divided in given ways. It also is constituted by specific opinions and preferences that are predominant. Yet, *as facts* this information is meaningless and devoid of structure. For example, it is impossible to understand in a meaningful manner the economy of a society unless we see the antecedent state out of which and because of which it was created. In a word, it is necessary to turn to history in order to understand the structure of a society. The roots of social relations are found in the past even as those of the future are found in the present. "Society is not separable from history; its mode of existence is to exist historically, and not only in the sense of being-in-history but in the sense of making and constituting itself in the very historical movement."[5] This does not mean that the study of society is history, only that the structure of society must be studied historically.

It is necessary to avoid two errors, both exaggerations, if we are to understand historical reality. The first is the confusion of the historicity of human life with its temporality. Human life considered as individual is temporal, but only certain relations between individuals of different age groups are historical. What is necessary is that "present men" co-live with those men of "another time." The avoidance of the first error must not lead us into the second error, namely, that the nonhistorical but temporal life of the individual human has history added to it. Since the selfsame ingredients in our circumstances, which we absorb to make our individual lives, are themselves covered with a patina of interpretations that are residues from the way those in the past felt about them, individual life is historical in its very substance.

Once these two errors are avoided, the way is clear to grasp historical reality. The unit of historical study cannot be the individual since historical life is a form of co-living. Nor can it be the totality of human beings because humanity lacks, at present, a universal system of binding observances; that is, humankind is too structually fragmented in its co-living. We are left with the intermediate reality of overlapping and successive living-with, what Marías—following Ortega—calls a generation. It is a zone of fifteen years that consists of a system of facilities and difficulties, of aspirations and prohibitions, of convictions and doubts. It is this configuration of human existence that each encounters from his birth, making being a man in 1862 A.D. quite different from that in 1862 B.C. It carries one through life, accounting for the affinities between members of the same generation.

There is a profound connection between society and history. From the beginning of "my life" I find myself in a society whose structure of binding observances has an existence prior to me. In this sense society is instrinsically historical, and history is concerned with the co-living between men of different age groups. The consequence is the inseparability of the disciplines of sociology and history. "Without clarity in respect to the forms and structures of collective life, history is nebulous [falling into an irrational denial of meaning or into an empirical accumulation of deeds]; without basing 'sociology' on historical movement, it is a pure theory or a repertory of unconnected statistical data, which does not lead to an apprehension of the reality of structures and, thus, social reality."[6] The task, the only task, of sociology consists in understanding social phenomena from the standpoint of human life. The task of history is the same, yielding an analysis of historical reality as rooted in human life.

II   *The Structure of History: Theory of Generations*

There has arisen in the twentieth century what may be called an "historical awareness" of unprecedented proportions due to a greater sensitivity of our long historical past and a progressive quickening of the historical rhythm to yield an accelerated tempo of history. One of the results has been a greater effort to understand the concept of generations. Although for thousands of years the genealogical fact of generations has been recognized and utilized in world literature, as witnessed in Old and New Testament writings, and in the works of Homer, Herodotus, and Hecatetus of Miletus, the earliest attempts to bring intellectual rigor to the concept date from only about the mid-nineteenth century. The result was rather unsystematic, as seen in the writings of Auguste Comte, John Stuart

Mill, Justin Dromel, Jean-Louis Soulavie, Antoine Cournot, Giuseppe Ferrari, Gustav Rumelin, Wilhelm Dilthey, Leopold von Ranke, and Ottokar Lorenz.[7] The most penetrating and coherent results have been obtained during the first half of the present century, mainly through the efforts of Francois Mentré, Julius Petersen, Karl Mannheim, Eduard Weshssler, Engelbert Drerup, José Ortega y Gasset, and, under Ortega's influence, Pedro Laín Entralgo.[8]

As is to be expected, Marías considers Ortega's theory of generations the first worthy of the name, probably because it arose out of his general theory of social and historical reality and was rooted in metaphysics as a systematic conception of reality.[9] It is upon Ortega's contribution that Marías builds. The main points of Ortega's contribution are the establishment of the generation as a fifteen-year zone, and the distinction between things that change in society and society itself changing with each generation. That is, "approximately every fifteen years the *entire system* of binding observances varies, almost always very slightly," with the supplanting of one generation in power by another that has been preparing itself to take over power.[10] It is Marías who connects this elemental unit of historical change with the empirical structure of human life, specifically with the mean duration known as ages. "That a generation lasts fifteen years is an empirical determination, valid only as a matter of fact. . . ."[11] Upon this generational change Marías bases what he called the macrostructure of history, namely, historical periods.

Almost all binding observances, although changing to varying degrees from generation to generation, remain in force for several generations. Some disappear but others become stronger or weaker. The important thing is that the majority persist. What Marías calls a historical period is a whole series of generations that base their lives on a given system of binding observances. The usual periods of history (antiquity, the Middle Ages, and the modern age) involve a principle that is not immediately clear. To clarify it we must know the function of the different types of binding observances involved and their relation to one another. Any change from one historical period to another involves an important modification of structure which can occur in two ways. One may be called a crisis of expectation, when man finds himself closed in without a future because the aspirations implied in his basic beliefs have been realized or are seen to be unrealizable. If the result is disillusionment, things are thought of as continuing in the same way indefinitely. If desperation results, there is a ray of hope because it is thought that things cannot go on as they are, and that in a short time things *must* change. The other way in which an important modification of the social structure may occur is by the innovative appearance of a new and important element, an element taking many forms, an example of which occurred with the discovery of the New World.

To determine the dynamics that occur in historical change in a given society, we must examine more closely the basic unit of structure of history, namely, generations. The discontinuous change that is history implies not only that there can be no historical situation in isolation from those that preceded and follow it, but also that each such situation involves a plurality of levels composed of groups of men born in various zones of dates. It is not enough to observe that generations succeed one another; it must be seen that at any one time more than one generation is living in dynamic interaction. In order for a historical situation to be intelligible at least four generations must be considered, involving approximately sixty years. In applying this to a study of a given historical epoch, with its distinctive basic beliefs, we must expand the generations to six in order to show how the generation that precedes the first differs and how the epoch ends after the fourth generation. Of the four key generations, the first attempts to impose something new on society, leaving it for the following generation that repeats and modifies it. The third generation appears when something new is predominant, while this predominant binding observance begins to weaken in the fourth generation.

As Marías readily acknowledged, it is anything but easy to determine specific generations. Generations belong to the analytical structure of individual and collective life, but precisely what they encompass is part of the empirical structure. To use the number fifteen is only an approximation, making it rather arbitrary when we attempt to delimit specific generations, for example, in the area of Spanish literature.[12] However, this should not lead us to be skeptical concerning the possibility of such, as human co-living is very complex. Because of this we have hardly begun the task of understanding history in terms of generations.

What is needed, as Ortega outlined, is the discovery of a decisive generation in which social change is greater than usual. This involves discovering its representative man, the beginning of whose public life, usually around his thirtieth year, yields the central date of his generation.[13] To accomplish this Marías proposes a method, a sort of "double entry" proof, that would take into account not only the mechanism of generations but our very ignorance of their specific dividing lines. The key to this method is to begin by making a list of a number of representative figures in different social functions approximately fifteen years apart. Next, we list the names of those in the same social functions who were born a year later. Most probably these will belong to the same generations. As we methodically continue our lists year after year we will come to a sort of boundary in which those born in this new year will exhibit differences too great to be considered of the same generation and will, accordingly, belong to the next generation.

According to Marías, this method has two undeniable advantages. One is its universality. That is, it can be applied to any period regardless of whether the generation is decisive or how difficult it is to locate the most representative individual. The other is that it is immediately effective. We are presented with representatives who necessarily exhibit the characteristics of their generations as well as the differences from other generations. Yet the method does have risks, including the difficulty of ascertaining generational represen-tatives, the limitation to approximately fifteen years, and the need to find individual lives in which the societal binding observances are evident. These risks can be avoided by beginning the empirical delimitation with a specific and undeniable society, within which several generations can be isolated, and by always connecting the generational traits with the various dimensions of the social struc-ture.

Leaving aside our own era, in which the situation of longevity is changing due to technology, we can say that at any given moment of time, three generations co-live or actually participate in the collective life of a society. They range from age fifteen to sixty. Before the age of fifteen, in the period of infancy and childhood, no historical activity takes place. What occurs is limited to private life. Until comparatively recently, those over sixty were too small in number to constitute a generation and act together, constituting survivors (often physically and mentally incapacitated) of a genera-tion that no longer existed. With increased longevity and social activity, the social structure is altering, and it will result in some kind of change of social roles; to what degree it is still too early to say. The generation between the age of fifteen and thirty, by and large, is being educated to take power. The one from thirty to forty-five is struggling to gain power and the one from forty-five to sixty is in power and struggling to stay in it. They do not succeed each other in the strict sense, for all are in power in some manner. Rather they overlap, like tiles on a roof, co-living by superimposition. All generations are contemporary since they live at the same time, while only those of the same generation are coetaneous since they are of the same age group. Generations manifest or express themselves through deeds that are social in nature and sufficiently exceptional so that they stand out or are memorable. It is not enough to investigate these deeds; they must be grounded in the substratum that gives them their reality, the underlying assumptions of binding obvservances that made them possible. These assumptions determine what needs to be expressed explicitly in contrast to what is merely implied because others of that time already know it.

The fact that history is an articulation between generations must not obscure the reality that all society is the articulation of a mass and a minority. This Marías accepts from Ortega, as seen in his mentor's *La rebelión de las masas* [The Revolt of the Masses]. In each case, of course, the articulation is reciprocal. The masses, quantitatively large in number, are organized and structured by a minority of a few select individuals. "Without the mass, there is no minority; the minority is the minority *of* a mass—and *for* a mass—; inversely, the life of a mass is impossible without a directive minority, . . . because without the interaction between the two, collective life is impossible."[14] When either the minority shirks its responsibility of directing or the mass is unwilling to follow direction, a once healthy society becomes sick and disintegrates.

These social functions of minority and majority do not necessarily coincide with the social estates or classes of society. Even when the guiding stratum of a society is the aristocracy, the qualifications of a minority do not pertain to each member of the aristocracy. Moreover, sometimes individuals from the lower stratum, even in the most stable societies, are able to reach positions of leadership, as seen in the bestowing of nobility and the rise in the ecclesiastical hierarchy. What confuses the issue is the qualitative, rather than quantitative, use of these notions, as when Ortega speaks of the mass-man and outstanding-man mentalities. In this sense, the mass-man mentality is not found among the masses only, representing as it does both the degeneration of the mass and that of the minority, and the outstanding-man mentality is not confined to the minority since it involves the effort to improve one's life rather than be mediocre by a member of any group.

What has preceded may be called the analytical theory of generations—what the concept means—in contrast to its empirical existence, to which we now turn. The historical evidence for the existence of generations is seen best in Marías's utilization of the concept in his numerous writings. For our purposes, the most informative use is found in Marías's presentation, in his study of Ortega, of the circumstances of his mentor's early life. If we ask into what sort of world was Ortega born, and at what time did he become a part of the happenings of that world, we are asking what was the generation that defined the ideas with which he had to deal and what was his own generational level. Of the Generation of 1826 only a few survivors remained at the time of Ortega's birth. Most of the members of the Generation of 1841 were still living when Ortega began writing. By the time he began his effective historical activity, this generation had lost power and gone into retirement. The generation really in power, the one with which Ortega has to contend, was that of 1856, a group that included Ortega's father and represented an ideal of intellectual discipline against which Ortega was to measure his personal and professional demands. The generation vying for power was that born around 1871, the group known as the Generation of 1898 because of the war between Spain and the United States. This group included Unamuno, and set the reigning ideas at the turn of the century.

Ortega, whose own generation was that of 1886, had strong affinities with the generation preceding his; he felt as though he belonged to it. His generation added its efforts to those of the earlier one, taking part in the same undertaking but with its own well-marked personality. It was not that the two generations agreed, for the differences between them were considerable, sometimes over serious matters. Above all, the younger generation was marked by a theoretical attitude while the older was characterized by a literary temper, explaining certain differences between Ortega and Unamuno. What there was between them was an accord based on a feeling that they were all participating in the same undertaking, the modernization of Spain. Since a generation consists, above all, in a commitment to an undertaking, Ortega's joining the commitment already in existence when he opened his eyes to the historical world meant that he felt a solidarity with his elders, devoting himself to continuing their basic beliefs. Using Ortega's own favorite word, he "adhered" to what they represented. His generation and theirs formed a sort of constellation.[15] According to Marías, Ortega was precisely the one who elevated Spanish intellectual life to a new theoretical level, to a form of theory it had never previously reached.[16]

III   *The Structure of Society: Theory of Binding Observances*

Society, like human life itself, is a vectorial system of directed forces with structures that are composites of dynamic elements. Stability continues for only short periods in a system of tensions between the binding observances of various generations, while those elements that appear to be unchanging are really enduring. The social structure as a whole is a historical movement, not in the sense of one structure merely succeeding another but in the deeper sense of the structure itself having a trajectory that is programmatic and exhibiting a plot. As such the trajectories manifest two essential ingredients, preservation and anticipation, that explain why all societies are to some extent conservative and innovative, with past and present appearing as tradition and originality.

As with human life, two kinds of structures compose society. One is the analytical, the prerequisites for any society, and is identifiable through reflection on our experience of society, while the other is the empirical structure that a given society happens to have. From an analysis of the very notion of the social, society is seen to be a co-living of men under a system of common binding observances. Empirical observation shows how this is accomplished in concrete societies. Co-living, for example, for the Athenians during the time of Pericles was not the same as for the Americans during the time of Eisenhower. The degree of seclusion of one society from another may differ dramatically as, for example, in the 1880s between the United States and Argentina with their vast immigration and Tibet with its closed frontiers. In each example the analytical structure becomes concretized only through the empirical, while the empirical is intelligible only by being rooted in the analytical.

At this point it is necessary to examine more closely what is meant by society's binding observances. The Spanish word for binding observances, *"vigencias,"* became a technical term in Ortega's social theory, appropriated by him from its usual use in juridical language. In that context, a law can be said to be "in force" (*vigencia*); it has the "force of law" or is presently binding. If a law is repealed or falls into disuse, it loses its vigor, becoming invalid or dead. When

Ortega adopted the word, he introduced, according to Marías, two new elements into the term. He freed it from its restricted use in the juridical sphere so that it could be applied in its full range, and he applied the word substantively to any reality "in vigor" or "in force." Thus, instead of saying that such-and-such is in force or binding, he spoke of a binding observance as a thing we encounter in our social environment, as a reality which must be taken into consideration because it is in force, has vitality, vigor, or strength. Those social realities that do not have to be taken into account, that can be ignored, are not binding observances.

Two examples utilized by Marías help to clarify the essential features of binding observances: the presence of vegetarianism and football or soccer. As it now stands, if I am not a vegetarian (nor is anyone close to me), it can be largely ignored. On the other hand, one cannot ignore the presence of football or soccer throughout most of the West. On the day of a key game the traffic is tied up by fans going and coming from the stadium, time is taken up on television, scores are inserted into newscasts and newspapers, conversations are devoted to it, etc. Football or soccer is a social reality that cannot be ignored, with which each of us must come to grips, requiring a stand for or against. Football or soccer affects my life, like it or not. If I like it, I do not feel forced to put up with it, even though the "force" of football or soccer is just as real to me as to one who does not like it. However, it is disagreeing with an observance that is the best proof of its binding nature, for under that condition it exhibits just how resistant it is to change and how coercive it is in its presence. This disagreement clearly illustrates that the mode of existence of a social reality is not simply "being there," but consists of exerting pressure and coercion, of inviting and seducing, that is, of acting on us. This acting is not the doing of something but is accomplished by merely being present, like a wall that blocks my way, if I disagree, or an opening that facilitates my passage if I agree.[17] A misconception must be avoided, however. The taking of account of binding observances must not be interpreted as necessarily a conscious and explicitly expressed action. With the exception of the instances when a binding observance is not fully accredited or when I personally deviate from it, I am subject to its power automatically, as to the law of gravity. Even as I do not usually think about gravity, automatically not leaving a book in midair, I expect cold water when I open the tap marked as such.

An aid in understanding binding observances is the fact that they have what may be called boundaries. If the boundaries extend throughout an entire society, the binding observance is general; if not, it is partial—keeping in mind that social units are not always the same as political ones and not nearly as rigid. No society can be defined by a single binding observance, for even basic binding observances come in skeins that intertwine. The general binding observance in the Spain of the Hapsburgs, for example, was that the Catholic religion was mandatory, an observance that included and excluded many other observances in that society. Partial binding observances do not apply to the entire society, as in regional societies such as Catalonia or Andalusia in Spain. In such insertive societies the majority of the observances that bind are felt as originating in a larger society. Apart from the geographical delimination of a partial binding observance, it is much less clear how to determine such, except in the extreme case of castes in which one group of observances bind to the exclusion of another. Some observances are binding only on one society (group or sex), but must be known by others so as to prevent social friction.

Taking into account binding observances must not be interpreted as meaning we must *either* submit *or* dissent. If I do not practice the Koranic ablutions, there is no dissent involved if it is not the prevailing custom of my society. On the other hand, if I do not wear mourning attire—remember that Marías is writing in the Spain of a quarter of a century ago—my decision strikes a violent note. It is only in rebellion that a binding observance is put to the test, that I experience just how much I am bound. Some societies even have a binding observance that compels us to tolerate dissent, not seeing it as a real threat. The normalcy of toleration of dissent is a good barometer for judging the stability of a society, indicating it is healthy and flexible. The fact that without dissent prevailing observances are usually not even known illustrates the further fact that they make their presence felt in two ways: explicitly and implicitly. The weaker the binding power the more explicitly known, as with laws, which have no force without the state and its police. On the other hand, the strongest, soundest, and most deeply rooted binding observances do not even appear as binding at the time. They are taken for granted, becoming visible only after their disappearance, or to a perceptive outsider exempt from them. The fact that men unreflectively react to binding observances is part of their reality. As soon as men realize that they are reacting, in the sense of conceptualizing the observances, the automatic binding power is gone.

Like human life itself, binding observances come to be, decline, and disappear through replacement. In other words, they have an age, even as do men. Originally the content of each binding observance came from an individual, being his preferences expressed in an action or in refraining from an action. At that point it was not binding. It became so only when a number of sufficiently key indiviuals in a society frequently began doing or not doing the same thing, so that others felt "one" ought to comply. It is not the frequency of complying that produces the binding observance; rather, it becomes frequent because it is binding.

Once launched, a binding observance exerts its pressure with varying intensity for a more or less given period of time, finally weakening in pressure and disappearing. The decline is not due to isolated individuals, even if they constitute a majority. The individuals must act as part of society, either as a majority or as a significant minority. The cessation of binding observances takes place in two ways: by dissolution or replacement. Dissolution means that the binding power decreases until there is none. It becomes easier and easier to break the rule, and the reprisals of society are milder and milder until one is free to do as one pleases. The usual case, however, is replacement as, for example, when the binding observance to duel for certain offenses did not lead to a situation where one is free to duel or not, but to another equally binding observance that forbids dueling under any condition.

IV *Belief and Lanugage as Binding Observances*

The necessary link of binding observances with men is seen, especially, in belief. Marías's use of the word is based on Ortega's distinction between beliefs and ideas,[18] a distinction that he considers to be one of his mentor's major contributions to both metaphysics and sociology. In a very real sense, ideas and beliefs exclude each other, even if the connections between them are many. Above all, both are found coexisting and functioning in our life and determine a series of characteristics of any specific way of life, including the rhythm of its historical change.

Beliefs have a mental existence only when formulated, especially the basic beliefs that are the distinctive interpretation of any given society. However, then they do not act as beliefs but as ideas. (Some ideas come from beliefs, but less rarely do basic beliefs issue from ideas, as the nineteenth-century belief in progress came from the eighteenth-century idea of it.) Otherwise, beliefs exist as unthought, simply acting as basic binding observances. We do not have them as we do ideas, but they sustain us. We are in them, kept afloat and carried along by them. Or, if dry land is preferred, they are the continents upon which we live and make our lives. As such, they can be revealed only by their effects. Concrete basic beliefs are the unformulated conditions and assumptions for the ideas, utterances, and acts of the members of a given society. They are seen best after they are gone, like an invisible boat of which one sees only its wake.

Ideas originate to supplement or complete beliefs. No more striking example of this can be given than medieval philosophy completing medieval theology, sometimes spoken of as philosophy acting the part of the handmaiden of theology. This is why the history of philosophy as a history of ideas *only* is incomplete and unintelligible without any underlying biography of philosophy, wherein is seen the change in basic beliefs through a change in what men have considered philosophy to be throughout its history.

Beliefs must not be confused with opinions. Like ideas, but unlike beliefs, opinions are overtly expressed. A person has an opinion like an idea, but any specific opinion is one of several possible opinions whereas an idea is not of this nature. A student could hardly answer the question on "What is the date of the Battle of Lepanto?" with an opinion. He either has an idea of the correct date, or he does not. Some topics have an "opinionability" about them while others do not. The function of opinion, both private and public, as a component of society is as an indicator of what the society considers worthwhile. Even if all the members know of an opinion, it is not public unless given in a public forum and meant to be "a matter of record" in some way. Men can have opinions on beliefs but beliefs as binding observances are much too strong to be considered opinions.

Categories of examination suitable for ideas are not appropriate for beliefs. The degree of importance of a belief does not depend mainly on whether it allows a broad and deep understanding of reality, as with an idea, but on its decisive effect on life. The soundness or solidity of a belief is not a matter of proof or evidence, as with an idea, but is whether it is implanted in basic levels of individual and collective living in order to exert its pressure. The connection or relation between beliefs is not one of logical consistency, as with ideas, but of systematic links of "vital foundation" they produce in human lives, the "enlivement" they produce in actions as men seek to fulfill their aspirations.

Even as aspiration, aim, project, or program is a proper feature of human life, so it is of collective life, launching both into the future through a process that involves imaginative construction of possibilities. Without erroneously giving a collectivity an independent life of its own, we can meaningfully speak of present-day Israel's aspiration as the "Chosen People," or of sixteenth-century Spain's project as a missionary people to the New World. (Often a society's program for collective life is discovered indirectly through conceal-ment in its literature and its licit as well as illicit "felicitary occupations.") Individuals within these societies may not personally feel such callings, but these aims must be taken into account by them since the societies are geared toward their realization. This does not mean that individuals' personal aspirations are determined by that of their society, but only that they must freely set their own within this context, where vocations and professions serving the collective end have a certain priority and privileged position.

If freedom is tied negatively to the absence of external coercion, it is linked positively to aspiration, which is not the same everywhere and at all times. Freedom is not opposed to all pressures but only to that which impedes us in realizing our aspirations. In this sense the absence of freedom appears as an internal contradiction in any society that suffers it. Freedom is a constituent of authentic collec-tive co-living. It is not something that a people or a person has; like life itself it must be continually made. Only an unhealthy society permits a state to usurp all freedom, as in a totalitarian situation. The state is an instrument of society, one of its components, and has the right to exert control over society only in restricted matters. During the last century and a half the state has grown tremendously, increasingly intervening in all social strata to lessen a society's vitality. A society keeps from going stagnant only if there is a balance between public power and social forces. If public power is too strong, social forces are snuffed out, while if it is sufficient, they are channeled. But, if public force is too weak, social forces act spasmodically.

Two of the key possibilities upon which the realization of the aspirations of the individuals of a society depend, collectively as well as singly, are classes and the economic system. Individuals are installed in society in more or less defined classes such that they feel "at home," even though there may be limited access to other classes, unless a caste system prevails. A class is a pattern of life whose guiding principle is the most relevant element at the time of its inception, be it religious, racial, ancestral, economic, or what have you. As a result, classes are finally justified not by privilege but by the specific and irreplaceable function they perform in a society. The important factor is not the heirarchy of classes, but that each is seen in comparison to others with its members living in view of other classes. "Naturally, this hierarchical order does not authorize any disdain for its elements, let alone the considering of them as expendable, for it exactly excludes these possibilities."[19] Each class needs the others in order for the entire society to function.

What is more relevant about a society than its total wealth, always to be understood in comparison with other societies, is its internal distribution and control. Also revealing are the accessibility of wealth and the degree to which it is linked to social status. The standard of living of a society constricts or facilitates the aspirations of its members. Regardless of how the economic situation appears to others, the important thing is how secure and happy the people of a society feel. Factors bearing on economic happiness include what is free and the attitude toward ownership and enjoyment of possessions, especially necessary luxuries. What must be kept in mind in studying a society is that quantitative figures are, at most, the starting point because we are dealing with human life.

Language is an excellent example of binding observances, intimately connected with a society's basic beliefs since it is the primary manner in which each individual is socialized. Language, a particular tongue, is the fundamental manner in which reality is interpreted in a given society. Rather than viewing language as a neutral mode of communicating about the world, we must see it for what it is, a means by which we evaluate our experiences. The reality of any language, like every element in society, is inseparable from its history. Language, too, is a vectorial system of forces, precisions, and tensions oriented from the past toward the future. So great is the parallel between a language and a society that if we trace a given language back in time—Spanish, for instance—we lose that society once we no longer have the language. Spain cannot be said to have existed beyond approximately 1,000 years ago when what might be called Spanish was used to write the "Glosas Emilianenses," those marginal commentaries composed by a bilingual monk able to communicate in Latin and in some form of Spanish.[20]

CHAPTER 5

Books on Countries: Forms of Co-living

I *Countries as Circumstantial*

JOURNEYS have played an important role in Marías's life. In his words: "There are places and countries that oblige me to write about them."[1] Despite the fact that some of the places that he visits are dear to him, Marías is not moved to write anything at all about them. Others about which he writes he has visited years before. Then there are those that he feels he must write about immediately, while the first impression is still fresh with him. Why? There are several reasons that appear to add up to a feeling of something unique that must be communicated before it fades away. Into this category can be placed his reflections on the United States, India, Israel, and parts of Hispanic America in his foreign travels, and his essays on the regions of Spain known as Catalonia and Andalusia. Together these writings constitute what Marías has called his "books on countries," which concretely illustrate the forms of co-living that comprise his theory of society.

The method used in these writings is a combination of impressionism and analysis. If the essays are composed immediately, it is a matter of telling what one sees as he is seeing it, without forgetting that one sees not only, or even primarily, with his eyes. Fundamentally one sees and thinks with his life, with his particular biography. As a newcomer to the United States, for example, Marías was seeing the country through the Spanish eyes of the young professor he was. But, more importantly, Marías was attempting to experience every word he heard, every thing he saw, all he found, against the background of American life in order to let it express itself as part of that life. In other words, he was letting things speak for themselves by placing them within their proper context, ultimately within their country as their circumstances. Without the methodological aspect of impressionism each thing would become abstract, uprooted from its circumstances, the residue of fleshless speculation operating in a vacuum. The absence of analysis would make things deceptive, so that we would run the risk of mistaking the peripheral for the constitutive elements.[2]

While still a young man, Marías realized that things encountered during one's journeys must be permitted to show their own truth, and he has carried this conviction throughout his many years of extensive traveling. In the journal he was required to keep as a condition for joining the 1933 summer cruise of the Mediterranean organized by the Faculty of Philosophy and Letters of the University of Madrid, he observed: "When something matters very much to us [so that it catches our attention], it is almost always because it touches us deeply, personally, and affects our very being."[3] Indeed, "[things] affect us to the degree that they and we have a common being, and that which touches us profoundly does so because it has a basic affinity with our spirit."[4]

This was certainly the case with Athens, definitely the high point of his trip, for the spirit of the young man. The young student of philosophy shares with us his thoughts and feelings as night overtakes him standing in the Old Agora, the ancient square of the city that served as both meeting and market place.

During these hours I feel more attached than ever to the city I am going to loose, and which matters most to me . . . . Never have I felt the meaning of Hellenic life so close to me in Athens as in this quiet and turbid hour in the Agora. This is irrational and absolutely inexplicable; but it is so . . . . Probably in the daylight the Agora would not give this feeling. But darkness lets us avoid a brusque encounter with things and reduces to a minimum that which is given to us externally; thus the spirit is able, with scant pretext, to project something essentially of itself into things and easily to find itself in them.[5]

Yet, Marías realizes, as he departs from Greece to Italy, that he really will not be leaving that life. For one sees ancient Athens through its architectural influences, even in Madrid; and we are close to Hellenic life through the writings of Homer and Aristotle. We carry the Hellenic civilization within ourselves through our cultural heritage as Westerners.

In words similar to those he would use approximately thirty-five years later in the lead essay of his second book on the United States, Marías points out: "In order to see it is not enough to open one's eyes. One must look, and this can be done well only when one moves within a horizon that is more or less previously known; one must bring to the viewing a prior outline of the nature of the objects with which one will become united."[6] That is, our biography must include some knowledge of what to expect or our experiences in traveling will be chaotic. Yet, our previous knowledge must be open to verification or correction as things show themselves. Although things do show themselves, we are only capable of interpreting them through our lives, the result being as much a revelation about the things and people we encounter as it is about ourselves.

After travels that involve reflection on our experiences, our lives are never quite the same, for our souls have been touched. If the individual involved is a philosopher, his viewing during his travels will reflect this. "Philosophy . . . augments the consciousness of living. It excites the senses, exacerbating the essential human possibilities of paying heed to things one experiences. It gives an almost morbid eagerness of seeing, in that deep sense of paying heed to life itself. It always arduously keeps open the eyes of consciousness."[7] Moreover, philosophy enables us to systematize all we see into a compact unity. The numerous ramifications that seem to exist independently of each other are seen as joined and bound together. The key point is that philosophy gives life the directive to see the radical meaning in the truth of things. The things viewed serve to springboard us back into our lives. After all, the trip during which we discover new or familiar things is something fleeting and mobile. It soon ends as a more or less lengthy and tiring leap. What matters is that the things experienced and the people met put us in contact with ourselves. It turns out that the meaning behind what is seen is within me, in my very being insofar as these affect me.

The importance placed by Marías on knowing the truth of things, and thereby knowing one's self more fully, must be understood in the context of the significance of the concept of circumstances in his theory of human life. Marías accepted Ortega's basic position that "I am I and my circumstances," and if I do not "save" my circumstances, I cannot "save" myself. That is, unless I look for the meaning of what surrounds me, I will not discover what I must do to make my life meaningful, how my circumstances offer the possibilities with which I create my life. Circumstantial reality forms the other half of my person, so that through it I can integrate myself to become fully myself. The world "stands around" us like a suit of clothes that we have worn since childhood in a very precise manner.[8]

This position was expressed explicitly for the first time in Ortega's first book, *Meditations on Quixote,* whose aim was to treat Cervantes's *Don Quixote* within its proper context or circumstance. That circumstance is seen to be primarily Spain, for "the individual cannot make his way in the universe except through his race because he is submerged in it like a drop of water in the traveling cloud."[9] By race Ortega meant, according to Marías, an historical manner of interpreting reality, an original version of human living and speaking. In attempting to understand any people, as Marías did in his travels, we must begin by trying to understand the things and places that silently stand around them, as these both form their lives and are formed by them. These "things" may be external objects or internal beliefs and ideologies within the psychic structure. As such, "[circumstances consist] . . . in the totality of those things that I find surrounding me and which I have to take into account, whatever they may be . . . and which are not *irreducible* to me in principle or absolutely, but without which I am not."[10]

II   *Traveler vs Tourist*

In all his trips Marías has attempted to journey as a "stranger" rather than as a tourist, a distinction he considers most important. Since the end of World War II, foreign travel has increased greatly so that it is no longer uncommon to find people from other countries traveling in most of the Western nations. What makes the greatest majority of these visitors tourists rather than travelers is that their journeys are so preplanned that their lives are closed to the unexpected and spontaneous, and they arrive back home basically the way they left. The contemporary tourist annuls the condition of "strangeness" that was previously more common in travelers. Those coming from different societies are "the other," par excellence, to those in the society being visited. As such, the traveler, with his ways distinctive of a society other than theirs, is strange to the inhabitants of the host society, strikingly pointing out to them their own unique manner of co-living. Adopting a distinction made by Ortega while traveling in Argentina in 1939, Marías contrasts travelers with natives of a country by pointing out that the stranger is he who *comes and goes* rather than he who *is* in the society. On the other hand, the tourist is neither in the society nor passing through it. He really is still in his own country because he is touring with a group of people much like himself. As a consequence, he fails to make contact with the new society and its people. (That is why Marías does not consider his earliest trip, when he toured the

Mediterranean as part of a summer cruise with fellow students, as significant as his later ones.)

That which is outside his planned tour does not interest the tourist, thus closing himself off from new experiences. Rather than interrupt his everyday life and substitute new experiences for the usual ones, as does the traveler, the tourist suspends his personal life, at the most, for an impersonal tour. The true traveler is he whose disposition is to be agile, porous, open, in order that many things might happen to him, things that usually do not occur in his daily existence. This is why the enjoyment that comes from suspending a certain form of daily living, and being open to the new, is so great for the traveler in contrast to the tourist. While the traveler vacates his usual life, to yield a vacation in the literal sense, the tourist is he to whom nothing really personal happens. Of course, tourism has its good points, and not much is needed to correct its worst defects. One is that tours must be arranged better so that people experience the things of the country visited. It seems that the more a tour costs, the less the tourist really travels—the high cost providing for a continuation of the things to which he is accustomed in his own homeland. Moreover, he is subject to the conventional and stereotyped on his guided tours, giving him a collection of fictitious experiences that prevent his really being in the very country he is paying to visit. Tourism must be less organized in order to leave room for chance, surprise, newness, to permit the individual to be alone and more on his own, to discover the true monuments to the societies he visits—its cities and their people. Only in this way will both the visitor and the visited benefit from mutual contact, a contact necessary for a friendship that is more than mere coexistence, that is truly co-living.[11]

With the exception of his two trips to Portugal in 1944 and 1945 to see Ortega, and a journey to Paris in 1949 to attend a philosophical conference, Marías's first travels after the Civil War were to Hispanic America. In the spring of 1951 he visited Peru and Colombia for the first time, returning again and again to that part of the world so that Hispanic America has become a part of his life that cannot be ignored and that he loves. As a writer Marías considers the region part of his public, keeping it in mind when putting his words down on paper, not because he writes in Spanish but because he is read by the people there. He prefers to call the region Hispanic America rather than Latin America, although he would like to revive the old expression "Las Españas" ("The

Spains"). This includes Brazil, which Marías visited for the first time in 1954 to attend an international congress of philosophy, for its problems are very much those of Spanish America, its cultured middle class reading Spanish without difficulty and as a second language.

Marías's first reaction to Hispanic America was one of stupor, of not believing his own eyes at the vastness of the region, of disbelief that the early Spaniards could have traversed the high mountains, raging rivers, and dense jungles. After his second trip, with most of the time spent in Argentina, Marías suggested in 1953 that Spain might act as the *Plaza Mayor*, the meeting place or area of co-living, of Hispanic America. He was promptly misunderstood. Two years later he attempted to clarify what he meant, pointing out that he did not say that Spain *is* the *Plaza Mayor* of Hispanic America, but that it *could be*. Moreover, he continued, he certainly never implied that, as such, Spain would be the capital of the Hispanic world, for that suggests the giving of orders. That a city, for example, Paris from 1815 to 1914, can act as a *Plaza Mayor* is another matter. If Spain earned the right to act as such, it would not only cease to be provincial in its outlook but become a meeting place in which those who speak Spanish could engage in dialogue.[12]

In an interview many years after the controversy, Marías stated: ". . . Spain is no more than a part of the Hispanic world. Hispanic America cannot be understood without Spain, as Spain cannot be understood without Hispanic America. We form a reality greater than any one of the nations that comprise it, which is the Hispanic world, which is [truly] a world. It is a true world because it is a repertory of usages—beginning with language—of beliefs, of ideas, of difficulties of various hues, of course, diverse in respect to each of the individual nations."[13] Yet, it is impossible to speak of Hispanic America as a society in the strict sense. Although Hispanic America's unique condition seems to call for the creation of a new society original to it, and authentically its own, this has not been the case even though from the *inside* the region appears more like a unitary society than different foreign countries. This paradox presents a difficulty that causes Marías to speak of the area only with timidity, despite his many years of interest in the region, various visits and lectures, and innumerable personal contacts.[14] This also includes Puerto Rico, whose uniqueness resides in the fact that it is still Spanish in culture and language, rather than bilingual, despite the fact that it has been under American rule since 1898. The University of Puerto Rico, where he taught with a Rockefeller Grant, has more decisive influence on the society of the island than any other university in any other society he knows. The historical soul of Puerto Rico's society can be discovered only by considering what it has been—in turn subject to the American politics of assimilation and isolation—*and* what it wants to be.[15]

In the fall of 1951 Marías made his first academic trip to the United States. In his words: "It was a case of love at first sight, what in Spanish is called *un flechazo* [a shot with Cupid's arrow] and this despite the fact that I was persuaded that I was not going to like the United States at all."[16] It seems that the impression Marías had received of the country, from a lecture he had heard the previous year in Paris by a native of France who had spent years teaching in New England, was completely wrong. He immediately discarded it, and resolved to see things for himself.[17] As he wrote years later, "I took in everything voraciously, feeling my soul was expanding, that I was beginning to be something more than I had been up till then. When I opened my eyes wide, not letting any synthesizing interpretation get between me and the things I saw, something new and irreducible came into my life: I felt that from then on I was not going to be wholly the same person."[18]

Coming to the United States was a decisive experience in Marías's life, for from that time forward the country was one more factor in his work. He thinks his life would have been quite different in certain respects had he not come, and that it would have been an error to have decided against it. As a result of his firsthand experience, Marías's ideas are essentially unlike those of most of his non-American contemporaries. Since the United States is the "prow" of the Western world, to be in error concerning it is to be mistaken about the state of the world itself.[19] To American society, strictly speaking another world to Marías, he owes much. In his words: "When I went there for the first time, I already had spent a few years reflecting on the problem of what society is, of what is the structure of society. The book entitled *The Structure of Society* that I was able to publish at the end of 1955 was born of my profound experiences of the United States as seen from Spain, of a constant comparison of social structures so different that they permitted me to see that very [structural] reality that had previously escaped me."[20]

From the beginning, the "friendship" which Marías struck up

with the United States was the means through which he attempted to interpret the Americans to the Spaniards, and vice versa.[21] Marías's collection of essays filled two volumes, and were based on experiences he underwent as he criss-crossed the country teaching and lecturing at large and small universities and colleges, famous centers of learning and the not-so-outstanding. With only one course in English behind him, he struggled to learn the language, and has come to be quite fluent in it. It is evident that he finds teaching American students, during their studies in Spain or in their own country, very stimulating. Despite the fact that the United States has "happened" to him because he has truly "lived" here, Marías does not feel himself to be an American, or even Americanized; he has never ceased being a Spaniard and a European.[22] Although he considers human reality, individual or collective, to be somewhat opaque, Marías is confident that he has detected the "intimate meaning" of the United States, as seen filtering through the expressions and gestures of its people.[23] Rather than finding life in the United States hectic, as he had anticipated, he finds it rather calm. The threatening danger to him is not the crowds but loneliness, probably because of the primacy of the private over the public life in this country. Most impressive to Marías has been the level of general morality, a level that includes a striking disposition toward benevolence with an infrequency of envy, that makes possible effective forms of co-living.

Because of the vast structural differences between Eastern and Western societies, Marías long thought he would have to experience India personally in order to make sense of the seemingly superficial and abstract information he had been hearing concerning the land. He eagerly accepted an invitation to participate in the joint meeting of the International Institute of Philosophy, of which he is a member, and the Indian Philosophical Congress in Mysore in 1959, spending three weeks traveling in the country during the monsoons, accompanied by an Indian friend. Hour after hour, he writes, he avidly absorbed India's sights, sounds, odors, and rhythms of life so that they could penetrate and saturate him. Would this be enough to understand the country? Certainly not! But experiencing is two thirds of knowing, provided the experience is not deformed by being forced into preconceived molds. If we permit the experienced reality to bring us its meaning, and lovingly go forth to meet it, our imagination can reconstruct even the forms of co-living in a society as far removed from ours as is the Indian of the Asian subcontinent. Since India is truly "other" than that to which we are accustomed in the West, it offers an excellent opportunity for expanding, and transforming, our own world.[24]

During the summer of 1968, Marías visited Israel at the invitation of the Israeli Academy of Sciences and Humanities. The nation was only twenty years old, and not recognized by the Franco government in its effort to befriend the Arabs. It must have galled partisans of the regime to read Marías's suggestion that Spanish become the second language of Israel, because of the fact that so many Jews speak Sephardic Ladino, as did Marías's driver during his motor trip through the country. The trip turned out to be one of the most powerful experiences in his life, deeply influencing his theory of society, and recalling the condition of the land when he had visited it during his Mediterranean cruise as a student. The reason for the society's profound influence on Marías is the uniqueness of Israel, a nation resurrected, with a general language hitherto confined to religious studies and ceremonies. Israel is not a "new" country, but a new state and society, for previously the Jewish people had not existed as a society and, hence, a nation in the modern sense. What they previously lacked in order to be a society was a land, what they believe is their Promised Land. No land other than Palestine seems to be able to take its place, the ancient land that the Jews lost but never forgot. There they have attempted to turn the desert into cities and gardens, to create a contemporary form of co-living.

One of the most important questions the trip left in Marías's mind concerns the ability of the Jews, for so long an urban minority in other societies, to transform themselves into both the minority *and* majority needed to constitute a society, dedicating themselves to farming as well as industrialization. Since this requires imagination, one of the principal riches of the Jewish people, as Marías sees them, it is his belief that they can reinstall themselves successfully in their new society. He found the "meaning" of Israel to be not only the liberation of the Jews, but also a sign of liberation of the rest of humankind from oppression similar to that which the Jews suffered. His hope is that the foundation of Israel can close the door on a sad chapter of anti-Semitism in universal history. Now that the Christians see no meaning in holding the Jews responsible for the death of Christ, Marías thinks it makes no sense for the Jews to hold the present-day Gentiles responsible for the mistreatment foisted upon their forebears by past non-Jews.[25]

III   Forms of Co-Living: Foreign Travels

As pointed out in the previous chapter, unless we view binding observances in a concrete society, seeing them as the real patterns of conduct of individuals living together that they are, and analyze their trajectories rigorously, our knowledge of the forms of co-living will be misleading. Some of the key structures of society about which Marías writes in his essays on foreign countries have been treated abstractly in the previous chapter. These include: basic beliefs, the dominant ideology and disagreement, wealth and the economy, entertainment and happiness. Other forms would have included education, friendship, cities, and death. Space limits us to a consideration of only two in the concrete: friendship and cities. The latter is especially important, as Marías considers cities to be the monuments to any society and its people.

Every individual encounters a certain number of people over a given period under varying degrees of closeness. Some are complete strangers, others are mere acquaintances whom we would never invite into our homes, while still others are very close friends. Friendship is an interindividual relation, conditioned by socially binding observances, based on intimacy and respect. It involves a certain amount of reserve, unlike what Marías calls love in the strict sense, for although friends feel comfortable together, there is no feeling of abandon. For this reason friendship is infrequent, the majority of relationships falling short of it or going beyond it. Usually it is between members of the same sex, since the normal birth of friendship between man and woman requires social conditions that rarely occur, although increasingly so during the last half century, particularly in America.

Indeed, Marías found that there is no more friendly or hospitable person than a North American, a discovery he emphasized again and again in his essays. Despite this, the United States is no paradise for friendship. The average American has few friends, seen infrequently, due to (1) the great mobility of the population (that destroys most intimate relationships developed during the key years of adolescence and young adulthood); (2) urban environments not conducive to frequent meetings; (3) insufficient time (the gravest threat to friendship today); and (4) television that stifles conversation. The one major factor conducive to friendship in the United States is the presence of a minimum of concord with the resulting trust, for when a society is deeply divided by political or religious ideology, wondering what the next person is thinking on these matters automatically vitiates and adulterates such intimate social relations.[26] In contrast, the major factor conducive to friendship in the entire Hispanic world is the physical presence of a centrally located square, the *Plaza Mayor*, to which people can come to see and be seen, to discuss and chat about current issues of mutual concern. Besides, Hispanics take pleasure in their *paseo* or stroll, thus being able to meet many more people out-of-doors without feeling obliged to invite them into their homes. Americans do not walk for pleasure, as Marías discovered in Los Angeles, a city of freeways and cars, where one has as much chance of meeting someone he knows as two atoms have of colliding in outer space.

It seems most Americans prefer to watch television, undoubtedly the most popular national pastime, curtailing much social interrelating.[27] Closely related to this is the Indian passion for the cinema. Motion picture houses are everywhere in India, while advertisements show that the movies are from all over the world. After Hollywood and Japan, India has the largest movie industry in the world. The lines for tickets, usually advanced sales, are long and the prices are anything but inexpensive. That the Indian needs, even more than food, a bed, and a house, the illusion presented by the movies is a point in his favor, as Marías interprets it. Movies are an art, but before that a drug, perhaps the most inoffensive one, bringing joy to the heart and expanding the horizons of life, giving us strength to endure the griefs of living. It is a credit to the dignity of man, Marías thinks, that he is willing to pay the highest prices for things that are almost unreal: a pinch of pepper, cloves, or saffron, a few leaves of tea, some coffee beans, a bit of tobacco, a few fleeting hours in the imaginary world of the cinema. Above all, the movies—and television, in its way—may provide the balance we need for much that is missing in our lives, including friendship. Paradoxically, the viewing of movies and television can also impede friendship unless there is a discussion of the experiences afterward.

A society is largely such due to its cities. In Marías's words:

I am particularly sensitive to the cities, to the ambient they reflect, to their physical makeup; cities are no more or less than the stage on which the drama of human life is lived. Cities and, naturally, their houses, are the stage for private lives and, above all, for intimate living. This is why architects seem to be such admirable people to me, for in their hands are found a great part of our destiny; this is why they have such a heavy responsibility; so heavy, in our times, in many places, that I would not like to have to share it with them.[28]

Since it responds to what the people in it do, a city is utilitarian, but at the same time it molds the life of the inhabitants. "To be born in a Mediterranean city, a South American one, a town in India, a Galician village in Spain, a great European city, already conditions what we will do, how and with whom we are going to relate, how we will divide our work and leisure time, our being alone and having the opportunity for association, conversations, and silence, and what will be the ways in which others will be present in our lives."[29]

Each city requires a relatively long time to become itself, expressing a style that reflects the deep sentiments of its people. As such, it is an open book to those able to read the workings of its spirit. Cuzco especially fascinated Marías in this regard. Its three epochs, the Inca, the colonial Spanish, and the contemporary Peruvian, exist side by side in more than architecture. The past is easily seen in the people and their everyday lives. Cuzco does not have a history; it *is* history, the only city about which Marías says this.[30] An individual lives in a city that he normally has not had a part in actually founding, even if he may transform or modify what he has inherited. Thus, cities are those aspects of our circumstances that play a key role in the making of our lives.

In seeking to understand a city, care must be paid to four characteristics: its size, degree of closure, internal structure, and social organization. In contrast to rural areas that are constituted by small numbers of people who know each other relatively well, cities are composed of people who hardly know each other at all. A city cannot even be called such unless it is a certain size, relative to the times and general population, and exhibits a certain diversification of professions and services. Beyond a certain size a city is really more than a city, the situation Marías says he observed in the United States. The larger the city the less its inhabitants know each other. However, this does not prevent American cities from having a lesser degree of what Marías calls "closure" than European or Hispanic American cities. By closure he means the absorption of a city in itself and its hostility to new ideas. American cities are the opposite of walled towns, open by a system of highways along which are signs saying "Welcome to X."

The internal structure of cities may be divided into cephalic, including polycephalic, or acephalic. If a city is defined by one center, a square or plaza, it is cephalic. Very large cities may have a number of these, exhibiting polycephalic traits, the many centers being merely topographic or implying a differentiation of functions. The majority of American cities are acephalic, having no centers that merit the name. Many American cities are connected with a main street, reminding one of a dorsal spine with vertebrae. Los Angeles struck him as an invertebrate, having no central portions or streets, and appearing more like a piece of interesting scenery composed of valleys, hills, ports, and beaches than a city. Some American cities even defy this classification. From the air the territory between Washington, D.C. and Boston looks like one gigantic city, especially at night, unlike the more sparse cities of Latin America and many European countries. These various physical features act as the scenery against which variations of the usual forms of co-living are acted out.

By social organization Marías means the urban distribution of social classes. Unlike the strict division of medieval and Renaissance cities, which were separated into sections by classes—the members of which met only in such places as the church or market, modern cities are more of a mixture. Chicago struck him for having factories next to luxury hotels, and trains running beneath its exquisite Art Institute. Even more mixed are the cities of India, mixed with the countryside, with luxurious buildings and homes side by side with hovels, not making it easy, as Marías sees it, to live in such a city, even though they are filled with life, activity, and hope, despite the miseries. At any rate, these cities manifest the form of life of old cities in ancient civilizations. The best way to describe the Indian is by the literal meaning of "civilized," a man for whom living is co-living, and this is evident in his cities teeming with people. The new phenomenon in the United States, by contrast with India a new civilization, is a city in which people work but in which few reside, the people living in suburbs—or residential cities—and commuting to work. As a result, American cities are less crowded at night, and less safe, than Spanish ones, for instance. Marías sees this trend to the suburbs as alarming, for the suburb as a fragment of life does not offer a place to live fully in association with others, something even small towns once did.[31]

Marías's short trip to Israel offered him the opportunity to see the creation of new cities. This is especially significant because the Jews were essentially an urban people in all countries in which they lived. The cities of Israel often exist side by side with the beautiful desert, unfortunately without enough modifications in their architecture to distinguish them from most newer cities throughout the world. Marías found Jerusalem to be a disoriented city. Its conglomeration of buildings led him to characterize it as "the history of an indecision." This is understandable since so many groups, always destructive, have passed through the city. What seems to be a unique creation of the Jews in co-living, neither a farm nor a city, is the kibbutz. This form of cooperative living for reclaiming desolate areas both mystified and repulsed Marías. He admits that he had had an erroneous idea of these collectives on which live nearly four percent of the population. Before his arrival in Israel he had thought they were all work camps in which mostly young people spent a few years. He discovered that those of all ages live there, that some are quite fanatical about their collective form of life being the wave of the future. Marías seems to have been distressed by the overly communal life, especially that children do not live with their parents.

IV   *Forms of Co-Living: Spain*

The reflections of Marías on his Spanish travels are seen mainly in his essays devoted to Catalonia and Andalusia.[32] They constitute excellent illustrations of the section in *The Structure of Society* dealing with regions within nations, those "insertive" societies characterized by a repertory of partial binding observances not extending beyond their borders into the greater society. The three very revealing features of regional binding observances indicate that they are: more voluntarily accepted (as one can move more readily to another region than emigrate out of the nation); more archaic, referring to life in bygone days (making regions traditionalist); and born of withdrawal from the society in general (usually giving rise to an attempt by the region to disguise itself as nationalistic to hide its derivative nature). As in so many other European nations, "[the] *concrete* mode of being a Spaniard is to be an Andalusian, Castilian, Catalan, Aragonese, Basque. . . . It is not easy nor likely that one could be a Spaniard 'directly.' In some cases it is impossible, specifically in the area of Catalonia."[33] There is nothing more anti-Spanish than the effort to diminish the personality of its regions; and to accuse their inhabitants of being less Spaniards than they should be is to commit a grave error. Spain, like all living social realities, is a unity of geographical and historical multiplicities, which gives rise to a fabulous plurality of possibilities. Those who misunderstand the delicate function of organic reality fail to see that a living unity can last only if it is agile, flexible, and mobile, and this requires a diversification, variety, and complexity that homogeneity excludes.[34]

Spain has nothing to fear from linguistic pluralism because it has a universal language that permits communication. However, for any region to opt for its language alone would lead to a kind of Tibetization of that area.[35] As a living unity of diverse regions Spain's future is assured if it adopts as its collective enterprise any one of three possibilities: to elevate itself to its proper level; to integrate itself into Europe and the West; and to act as the coordinator, the *Plaza Mayor*, of Hispanic America. If it adopts all three, as it very well could, Spain would gain a new greatness, one in which the country would develop *not* at the expense of others but *with* them and *for* them, as benefits the twentieth century.[36]

As is to be expected, one of the key realities in Catalonia and Andalusia to which Marías turns his attention is the city. He remarks: "The [different] forms of cities interest me more and more; it excites me to see how architecture, over century-long periods, has succeeded in expressing a form of life which is translated into the attainment of beauty. . . ."[37] On the other hand, he is dismayed that the lack of skill in doing so has been extreme during the last century. That is, for approximately one hundred years there has not existed in Spain, nor any place else, an adequate way of understanding a house and a city as collective means of installation. While the cities of Andalusia have succeeded almost miraculously in maintaining their beauty, some Spanish cities—harmonious and happy in their magnificent, modest, or even poor circumstances until 1850 or 1860—are now largely expressive of an arrogant frightfulness and arbitrariness, or of a vulgar and ugly spirit. "At times I think, standing in front of a recently built house, that the architect must have built it without ever looking at it from the sidewalk, but only at a manual or magazine that was delivered with the last mail."[38]

The cities of Catalonia exhibit three characteristics. First of all, they present aesthetically extreme examples, going from the most intense beauty to the most disturbing ugliness. In his words: "Each time I see beauty around me—in a house, in a city—I feel tranquil and hopeful; ugliness, on the other hand, jolts and bothers me, disturbs me and makes me fear for the worst, the invasion of an ugly spirit that operates under concealment waiting its moment to break into the open."[39] In the second place, the urban forms of Catalonia are private, geared to family living rather than to public life, offering their inhabitants the temptation to seclude themselves. Third, these urban centers manifest a harmony and a coherence, except for the Costa Brava (troubled with fast development), the area of Llobregat (with its unnecessary and dangerous ugliness, despite being one of the wealthiest in Spain), and Barcelona (a gigantic and unique world-in-itself).

Barcelona is one of the few cities of the world that is at least two thousand years old. It has preserved in a superlative manner its continuity with its past, not only by retaining its relics but by harmoniously building on what came before without rupturing its history. Its Gothic district is one of the capital treasures of Spain, extraordinarily beautiful and the best example of civil architecture in this style in all of the Pennisula.[40] Its size, dignity, and nobility of architecture give Barcelona a European flavor rather than merely a provincial or even a national one. However, it does not fulfill the double function of any great city as a form of co-living; to act as the stage for the territory, region, or country of which it is the head; and to be the representative of its historico-social reality in any dialogue with other areas. A great city cannot close itself off from others or it will end by not even knowing itself. The relation between Barcelona and Catalonia has been minimally reciprocal; the region gravitates toward the city but the city feels no obligation to the region. As a result, Barcelona does not live at the level it could, at the height of the times, even though it has good reason— in contemplating a projection of itself over the entire nation—to be suspicious of Madrid because of past politics.

Hopefully Barcelona will radiate its good taste outward to those industrial cities that have sprang up in its shadow. It is not necessarily true that industry is always accompanied by ugliness, that the emphasis on the utilitarian implies a disdain of beauty. It is only that the two became allies at the very beginning of industrialization when old forms could not be adapted to new functions. But those days have long since passed. Industry can keep these effects to a minimum today. There is no reason why the cities surrounding Barcelona should give the impression of forlornness. They look like they have fallen on hard times, as though their days were numbered and they were on the verge of being abandoned, despite the fact that they are some of the wealthiest in Spain. Other Spanish cities, still largely untouched by industrial pollution, are not like this, except for certain lower-middle-class sections of Madrid. Ugliness elsewhere seems to be provisional, while in these industrial centers it is constitutive, accompanied by an atrocious decline in good taste, a following of bad principles rather than the good traditions of artisans trained by masters.

The cities of Andalusia manifest its distinctive manner of being installed in life, an attitude of authentic integration within its circumstances. More than elsewhere the force of Ortega's words in *Meditations on Quixote* comes to mind: the reabsorption of his circumstances is the concrete destiny of man, a reabsorption that consists in man's humanization of his circumstances, in adapting them to his projects.[41] In Andalusia, the oldest land of Spain, the cities are ancient but still contemporary, in the sense that their houses, streets, and plazas still act as forms for authentic co-living, and not merely as relics. The symbol of Andalusia, for Marías, is the house that is whitewashed year after year to enable it to act as a continous and ever-contemporary form of co-living.[42]

Seville, the principal city of Spain for many years, manifests the fact that cities are those realities in which man most purely and intensely expresses the effects of collective living.[43] In walking its streets we can read its history. The culmination of its houses is the patio, more like another room of the house, the "within" par excellence in contrast to the open gardens seen in the small cities of the United States. The promise of the patio is shade, refreshment, intimacy, and rest—the opposite of hurriedness. This is especially evident in the *barrio* of Seville called Santa Cruz. All of Seville seems to portend, to promise, this section. When it is first seen, it looks unreal: all its details seem to be extreme, exaggerated, spontaneously and intentionally placed at one and the same time. The precise location of its flowerpots, grills, and lanterns, the names of its streets and plazas in tiles on whitewashed walls give it the aire of a theatrical set. Yet, it expresses the life-style of the Andalusians, one that has seductively captivated all who visit the region, one that has radiated itself across the waters to give the distinctive tonality to life and speech in Spanish America. It is little wonder that when others think of Spain, it is Andalusia that comes to mind, with its prosperity and tragic poverty, its strange intermixture of happiness and sadness, extending even, or especially, to its religious life. Indeed, Andalusia represents one of the highest life-styles which man has attained anywhere, an integration of man and his circumstances.[44] That Andalusian attitude toward life, despite all its drawbacks, is that "it is worthwhile"—*Vale la pena!*

CHAPTER 6

Philosophy and Literature

I *The Role of Literature in Education*

THROUGH the study of literature people more readily gain an interest in matters that otherwise might not appeal to them directly, including philosophy. Literature has been the greatest means of interpreting the various ways human life can express itself in history. By means of poetry, narratives, drama, movies, and—above all—novels, life becomes transparent to itself. "Fictitious narratives are like maps thanks to which we are able to know the structure of vital reality, and they give us a sketch of that which we are doing—living—and normally make possible the ability to project ourselves into the future."[1] Literature in this sense is part of the very condition of life itself. It is no wonder that literature has always been the instrument of humanization in great societies such as that of ancient Greece. Its *paideia* or education was a literary one, primarily the study of the Homeric poems and other forms of literature, rather than of philosophy and sciences which they discovered.

The everyday life of those people who have not left adequate literary works, such as the Visigoths of Spain, is opaque to later peoples despite other written documents. Without the creation of a literature, even societies that are materially prosperous and militarily mighty will exhibit a sterility that leads to their demise. For, above all, what will be wanting is the only means by which man can personally project himself into his creations. Human living as a constitutively projective operation toward the future must be anticipated imaginatively, obliging each of us to engage in the "poetic task" of becoming the novelist of himself, be he original or plagiarist. Moreover, interindividual and social relations are impossible without that ever-urgent projection that consists of imaginatively discovering the plans of those with whom we associate, and of anticipating their reactions to our plans, to create a sort of "novel of urgency."

Modern-day Spanish society has always been a literary culture. The very preservation and unification of Spanish society is possible only by literature acting as a sort of nervous system, if not the spinal column, so that the society senses itself as a national unity. To ignore literature as part of the educational requirements is tantamount to anesthetizing Spain, to alienating Spaniards from themselves so that they begin the march to their demise as a people. Even worse, it ultimately would destroy the transnational unity of Hispanic-speaking peoples whose literature, international as it is, is an effective counterbalance to the rampant nationalism plaguing contemporary times. If there ever was a universal literature, it is that of the Spanish language, rooted as it is in the Hellenic tradition, especially in Latin literature, and related to Germanic, Judaic, Islamic, and the Amerindian literatures. Spanish literature draws each country beyond its own national borders to participate in the cultural life of the others.

To de-emphasize or eliminate the study of literature is the temptation and trend of contemporary technologically minded societies, despite the fact that it undercuts the very purpose of higher education—to give the student an idea of *what* is that world in which he will have to live. It is a demonstrable error to believe that man lives only or primarily in a physical world, and that the study of the sciences suffices for the required world picture. The immediate world in which we live is the social world, one constituted by historical interpretations expressed linguistically. Language as the primary interpretation of reality is inseparable from literature precisely because these interpretations are already literary. If a formal literature is not created, a language suffers a privation that frustrates its development, since language "functions" in literature, unlike in grammar and in dictionaries. The dropping of literature as a general requirement in the educational system can only be interpreted as lunacy. For those who willingly agree to it, it is cultural suicide, while those who have it forced on them are culturally sterilized or assassinated.

This does not mean that literature alone is the instrument by which contemporary man can be humanistically formed. Philosophy, history, the arts, and the sciences are all indispensable and are not reducible to literature, which cannot even be studied without referring to these other disciplines. Of course, the reverse is also true, especially in regard to history and philosophy, because of the unique reference these studies have to the constitution of man. The drama that is the structure of human life orienting itself toward the future, that has a plot or "argument" that must be articulated both to itself and to others, would be unintelligible without a study of literature as a mode of knowing ourselves. This intrinsic dramatic structure of life is the main theme, the basic discovery, of great authors like Shakespeare.[2]

What is meant by the discipline of literature must not necessarily be taken for anything that goes by that name. We have only the beginnings of what might be called a history of literature, the manner in which most are introduced to its study. The humanities need even more time than do the sciences to become disciplines in the best sense of the word. One cannot present an adequate history of literature merely by giving a list of authors and their works, and examining the origin, source, and antecedent influences of these works. This presents us only with the key starting point, the historico-social circumstances of the author. For all the importance a sociology of literature might have in determining the binding observances, including the prevalent literary genres, that a society imposes on an author, the main factor is what he does with them. Only by investigating this do we discover the originality of the author. "And this is the reason why we are interested in literature and why we study it, its value as such, primarily aesthetic; this is why we exert ourselves to investigate its structure, its origins, its antecedent conditions, its consequent effects."[3]

II   *The Novel as a Mode of Knowledge*

Every novel, in effect, is based on a certain idea of human life held by its author. This idea is usually not formulated by the author himself, but is absorbed from the predominant beliefs and ideas of his time and society. It may even be held in an unconscious and unclear manner. Such a factor is quite important, being manifest in literature for some time, even if books on the topic are silent concerning it. The so-called *romans à theses*, or "thesis novels," of the nineteenth century are an example. In them the already-known ideas of the characters are in conflict. Then came the psychological and naturalistic novels of the second half of the last century. The latter novel is really a literary extension of positivism, viewing human nature deterministically and reducing man to his psychic life as seen externally through his actions. Today psychic life is seen within its proper context of human life. The result is what Marías has termed the existential or, even better, the personal novel.

There have been three attitudes toward this new type of novel. The first was determined by the necessity of finding a new form of knowing human life because philosophy had not formulated one. Dostoyevsky, Proust, Pirandello, and, especially, Herman Hesse and Kafka were in the forefront here in objecting to the traditional novel in which life had meaning only apart from our conflicts or living it. The innovation of the new novel, without directly speaking of it in a theoretical manner, was to discover that life itself undergoes conflict in facing the problem of meaning. The second was the presentation of the novel as an autonomous method of knowing, as a substitute for philosophy that had been rejected as incapable of undertaking the life and death of man. Since human reason as operative in philosophy freezes and kills all it touches, paralyzing fluid and temporal reality into coldly rigid concepts, only the forms of the novel or the play can understand life. Unamuno is a prime example here, being the heir in his irrationalism to Kierkegaard, Nietzsche, James, and Bergson. The third, and last, was the discovery of the novel as a complement or auxiliary instrument of philosophy, as a paraphilosophical method. In many instances this kind of novel is linked to existential philosophy, to Sartre and Simone de Beauvoir and, in a certain sense, to Camus and Marcel. As a result, their literary works are incomprehensible apart from their philosophy.

According to Marías, Unamuno is the real inventor of this literary genre of the existential or personal novel. His novels are the oldest and best—and in a certain sense, the worst—examples of this form. Unamuno always exaggerates; for him life *is* exaggeration. With the exception of his first and last novels, this makes his novels defective. His novels are distinctive in that they contain no description, and give hardly any indication of place and time. He prefers to give only the bare bones of his characters, leaving the reader the task of imaginatively clothing them and endowing the novelistic personages with the ability to create themselves as they go along. In all his novels Unamuno is interested not in any single event in the lives of his characters, but in their very existence, in the depths of their very persons, whose sole problem—he contends—is human existence itself, whether man dies completely or is immortal. Unamuno's fictional creatures reflect him and his need to probe the experience of death and his desire to survive. Death is the absolutely most unique experience a man can undergo, since even birth is not an act of the person who is born, and its meaning is not diminished with the postulation of some sort of survival through immortality and resurrection. The only thing that can be done with death while we live is to anticipate it. To anticipate it is to see it imaginatively, to make it arrive and have it already present while we are still living. The novel can be this imaginative preliving, and with Unamuno all his works are a *meditatio mortis*, a contemplation of death.[4]

Contrary to Unamuno, Marías maintains that the novel cannot satisfy all the demands of the strict knowledge necessary to give us the truth of human existence. Certainly the novel takes place in time and has duration, as does life itself. It can capture what description alone cannot give, the very rhythm of life. Yet, narration, which is the essence of the novel, is only one mode of living. What it omits are the assumptions of what is being narrated, the meaning or concepts behind the narration. The novel does not possess any mode of conceptualization of its own. For this it must rely on philosophy itself. Life can only be narrated in terms of conceptual categories that reveal the modes of human reality. Moreover, the novel leaves large areas of human life in shadows to concentrate on others, arbitrarily breaking up reality. This is the root of its exaggeration. This limitation would be acceptable and cause no danger if it were undertaken consciously, but in a novel this does not happen, thus yielding a certain falsification, if only because it omits indicating how each part complicates the other due to the systematic nature of reality. Even the personal novel can never be the primary and autonomous mode of knowing. Its assumptions are not the conscious ideas of philosophy but the unconscious beliefs of the collectivity of that particular time and place.

The most productive function of the personal novel from the perspective of philosophy is as a preliminary step to metaphysics. "It can put us in contact with the very reality that we must describe and [later] conceptualize metaphysically."[5] In this sense the personal novel functions fully as a method, yielding a preliminary intuition of human life working itself out in all its richness and plasticity, the very point of departure for all philosophy as metaphysics. As phenomenology has shown, it makes no difference whether those intuitions are of fictitious or actual realities in yielding their essences to our analyses. The novel, including drama and the movies, gives us an abbreviated form of life, making it less opaque. It also permits us to experiment with human lives as we cannot do actually. By a fictitious "experiment" we can get some idea of how a person might act, for example, when he unexpectedly inherits millions of dollars or discovers he has an incurable illness. Such experiments cannot be said to be without cognitive value, for fiction has some verisimilitude to life. In a word, the novel utilizes a kind of knowledge that is effective, even if not rigorously conceptual; it discovers and clarifies realities that later can be raised to a more rigorous study.

III   *Philosophy and Literary Genres*

The intimate relation between philosophy and literature is striking, especially, when we turn to the topic of literary genres in philosophy. The customary way of speaking of literary genres, as if they were containers in which their contents are poured, is dangerously misleading. So intrinsically bound up is philosophy with its literary genre that it would be more accurate to speak of it as incarnate in its literary form. Neither philosophy nor the genre can be conceived of as existing prior to, or independently of, the other.

Philosophers usually have adopted and adapted the prevailing literary forms of their times and places due to social pressures, rarely inventing their own. Likewise, the reader of philosophy in a given epoch has read philosophy written in other epochs from his own preference of genre. For example, those who consider the essay to be the proper vehicle of expression for philosophy, transpose the Parmenidian poetry and the Platonic dialogues into such. Only recently have we begun to appreciate that the particular literary genre must be respected in order to understand what is being philosophically expressed and to avoid adulteration, for the truth of any position is not independent of its form of expression.

The problem of literary genres in philosophy is mainly that of what the philosopher wishes to say, not in the sense of the concrete doctrinal content of each philosophy but as to what the statements mean to the philosopher, primarily, and to his readers, secondarily. For example, the philosophic genre of the Christian meditation, of which Saints Augustine and Bernard are outstanding figures, relates a spiritual itinerary personally traveled by the author and repeatable in principle by the readers. Again, the English essay of the seventeenth century not only relates the result of the investigation conducted "concerning" some theme or other, but presents the manner in which it is obtained.

The twentieth century has inherited the problems of the preceding century, but has failed to solve them adequately so that the crisis of literary genres in philosophy has grown. Our times have continued the inauthentic practices of adopting mostly the prevalent university pedagogical styles or imitating the sciences in their research. Those who succumbed to the temptation to turn philosophy into literature have acted as a counterbalance to turning it into science, but it was only a sort of first-aid bandage that prevented philosophy from bleeding to death. Only those who have taken philosophy itself to be a problem have directly faced the issue of literary genres, being at once creative and fully contemporary. But, none of these have succeeded in writing a philosophy book in the strict sense, one that acts as the appropriate literary vehicle for the theory expressed. Heidegger has shown an excessive dependence on the German language, while Marcel and Sartre, despite their creativity, have reproduced university manuals. In the English-speaking world, publications have been on very specific topics in imitation of scientific studies. Marías does detect the beginnings of an interest in the United States in what constitutes a book, but finds that this has had no effect on philosophy because of the relatively marginal position of philosophy, and the obstruction to creativity by the advisors that influence publishing houses or philosophy journals.[6]

In Spain, where the volume of philosophic publication is much less than in the other countries mentioned, the situation is rather unique. There we find an extreme case of preoccupation with literary genres, first by Unamuno and then by Ortega and the School of Madrid.[7] Since Spain lacked an immediate philosophic tradition acceptable to Unamuno and Ortega, they creatively sought their own, by avoiding the reefs of the Scholastic manual or textbook genre of Balmes and the German university forms of the Krausists. Unamuno, as Marías understands him, succumbed to the temptation of literature, but to such a high degree that he created something unique. More than representing philosophy in the clothing of literature, Unamuno renounced the very task of philosophizing and created his great masterpiece, the existential or personal novel. In the meantime he wrote *Del sentimiento trágico de la vida* [The Tragic Sense of Life], in which he irritatingly—to Marías—philosophizes about the impossibility of philosophizing, presenting his "negated philosophy" under the guise of poetry or mythology. On the other hand, Ortega committed himself to philosophizing by the use of vital reason, probably never writing a line—Marías believes—

without asking himself what he was going to say, whether he had to say it, to whom, and in what manner. In doing so he transformed the newspaper article and the essay so as to provide us with ". . . the most promising point of departure from which to reach a literary genre adequate to the philosophy of our times."[8] But even Ortega never wrote a book of philosophy in the strict sense; his publishers simply put together his various essays.

For many reasons, the problem of literary genres is especially acute today; these reasons can be reduced to three types: (1) the variation within philosophy over the last century; (2) the social situation or role of philosophy during this time; and (3) the very idea of philosophy and its most profound aspiration. Our century represents a real break with the dominant conception of philosophy in the last century. The result is that there is no prevailing or definitive philosophy today, let alone a reigning literary genre. This has forced philosophers to invent their own genres, especially if they write about themes that have never, or rarely, been written of before. This necessity of inventing a new genre is imperative if the philosophers are to communicate beyond an exclusively scholarly or academic circle. Philosophy has drawn the interest of a considerable number of nonprofessional readers in most Western countries, albeit to a lesser extent in the United States. With an audience different from the traditional one, the philosopher finds the expectations regarding what he is going to say quite varied. Whatever he does, he cannot avoid these expectations. "And this conditions, of course, the literary genre of his writings, because these are always the result of a collaboration between the writer and the invisible chorus of his readers."[9]

Despite the fact that there is no reigning philosophy today, Marías finds it *philosophically* unacceptable to leave the matter of determining the task of philosophy and its appropriate literary genre to the discretion of individual authors. It is the structure of reality itself that must be permitted to impose itself on thought, precisely what occurs when, in living, we have to give an account of reality, to give (or find) meaning or reasons for reality, in order to go on living. It is this situation that must determine our choice of literary genres. If philosophy is systematic, so that any one aspect implicates the rest, it is because reality is also. Literary genres must communicate this. In other words, a philosophy book must be determined by things themselves. Of course, things by themselves never write a book. It takes an individual sufficiently open to reality to do so. We must start with our encounter with things in the present, letting the real connections that we discover in our lives condition the coherence of our philosophical writing. The order and mode of exposition corresponds to the mode of our actual insertion in the real. Even as life as lived is an undertaking, so

> . . . a philosophical book is an undertaking. It is the expression of the dynamic vital situation in which its author finds himself. This means that a book of philosophy will have to be necessarily *dramatic*. From this follows, aside from the significance that the novel may have for philosophy, that a philosophic book, even the most rigorous theoretical study, must have a dimension of the novel. . . A philosophy book must be *more* than a novel, but never *less*, never lacking that which the novel contributes. . . . For what is being treated is not only, as one might be led to believe, the fact that the book expresses or narrates a certain adventure, but that the book itself is a personal adventure of its author.[10]

IV *The Dramatic Structure of Philosophic Theory and Metaphor*

Since philosophic theory is the taking of conceptual possession of human life, it must be faithful to the structure that constitutes that form of reality. The narrative outline (*argumento*) of philosophic theory makes manifest the dramatic plot (*argumento*) of life as an aspiration freely directing itself toward the future. If we examine the etymology of *argumento*, we find that it is derived from the Greek stem that means radiance, brilliance, or whiteness. The word "silver" also is derived from this stem, as that metal appears to be the substance that glistens, is white and brilliant, and has clarity. The Latin *arguo*, from which *argumento* in the sense of narrative outline or "argument" directly descends, basically means to brighten, to clarify, to illuminate. The original task of philosophical argument was to clarify things, to make them shine or manifest themselves, precisely the meaning of truth as *alétheia*. Philosophic theory is a technique of bringing out into the light what is latent, a reality developing along a preimagined but not preimposed plan, a development which is plotlike. In philosophic theory we articulate in narrative or story form the storylike occurrence of life, ascertaining its "why" and "wherefore."

The best way to illuminate the human situation is by the use of metaphors. Metaphor, as used in both philosophy and literature to clarify the human situation, reveals itself as a mental hook to grasp a reality that can be known in no other way. Of the two philosophers in our times who have discovered human life as the fundamental reality, Ortega and Heidegger, only Ortega chose to use a metaphor in narrating what was newly unveiled. Heidegger chose to invent a new term, a neologism, the danger of which is that we run the risk of failing to understand life and, even more, of mistaking the term for the reality.[11]

The role of metaphor in literature and philosophy is different from the use of old words to name new realities. In metaphors old words are used obliquely, with different meanings. It is like pointing a finger at something. Pointing something out is a suggestion that another person look in that direction and discover it for himself. Of course, there is always the danger that the person will look at the finger, the old word, instead of the new reality. "The philosophic metaphor suggests that we follow a certain line of thought so that we can discover what is intended. In philosophy metaphor is a mode of discovery," whereas in literature it is a means of aesthetic enjoyment elicited by a kind of identification of two terms.[12] The philosophic metaphor is not meant to be taken literally. There is need for some kind of transposition or translation while retaining the old meaning of the word. Otherwise the metaphor is lost, as in the case of "money." This English word and its Spanish (*moneda*) and French (*monnaie*) equivalents come from the Latin *moneta*. Originally *moneta* was a place in Rome where a temple to Juno was located, so that the building was known as Juno Moneta. The Roman mint was also located in this place, which gave its name to the coins produced. Since this is entirely forgotten today, the word cannot be used as a metaphor.

As we saw, philosophy not only discovers but interprets. Paradoxically, philosophy does not interpret by adding anything to reality but by discovering, through unveiling, that there is an interpretative character that belongs to reality itself. Among the tasks of philosophy is the removal of those interpretations surrounding the real things we come in contact with, interpretations presented to us since birth. When, in trying to reach reality, we peel away the interpretations, we find that reality is simply that which requires us to make interpretations of it. Marías believes that the universe is covered by a patina of interpretations, most of which are metaphors.[13]

In philosophy the greatest metaphor of all is "being." It is an interpretation of reality, and not fundamental or radical reality as most philosophers have maintained. In the philosophy of knowing, the two epistemological metaphors are those of consciousness as an "impression," the basis of realism, coming from the Greek experience of tracings on a wax tablet, and of consciousness as having a "content," the basis of idealism, coming from the modern experience of the container creating the "form" of the contained. Ortega challenged both, suggesting a third metaphor that would view subject and object as inseparably facing each other, like the Roman household deities, the twin sons of Jupiter, Castor and Pollux, who lived together. He also expressed this inseparable and irreducible union as Adam in Paradise. Both these metaphors are ways of stating "I am I and my circumstances." "Now we have a third metaphor, which may last a long time, or perhaps not [depending on how philosophy develops], but which will one day certainly be replaced by another metaphor, a fourth metaphor."[14]

Since the task of metaphor is to throw light on reality, to discover aspects of reality, and reality is a plurality of interconnected aspects, the metaphor that discovers one aspect is connected by implication with other metaphors that discover still other aspects. "A central metaphor integrates itself with other complementary metaphors, which in turn discover other connected aspects of reality. Therefore, the metaphoric approach to reality utilized by the philosopher is a never-ending process. Thinking cannot stop. The imperative of a vision is to keep on looking at things. There is an interconnection between metaphors that illuminate each other. And this is what I call the metaphoric system: metaphors that are linked together, and illuminate the different faces of reality."[15] Thus, we discover reality by following the intricacy of its metaphorical interpretations. If we speak of an original or central metaphor in a philosopher's position, we must not be deceived into thinking we have a formula that gives us the secret of reality, e.g., "Idea" in Plato, "substance" in Aristotle, the "cogito" in Descartes, the "monad" in Leibniz, the "Absolute" in Hegel—even "I am I and my circumstances" in Ortega. What the central metaphor does is trigger a whole set of connected metaphors that come to mind to aid us in penetrating reality in order to follow its intricate connections.

V   *Literary Criticism*

Marías's theory of literary criticism is interspersed throughout his various essays, each of which is a concrete example of the criticism of literature. Here, as elsewhere, he combines the intuitive qualities of impressionism with the systematic aspects of analysis. The result is a grounding of literature in human life, the viewing of literary works as possibilities of human living in its search for meaning and happiness. The metaphorical use of language in literature enriches the lives of those who read literature, making them less susceptible to cultural stagnation and propaganda manipulation. The reading of literature, like its writing, intimately affects our personal dimension, expanding the reader's vital horizons where he unveils the interpretation of reality offered by the author. In this way the serious study of literature, like any art form, helps us to reestablish and maintain contact with our inner lives. All art forms act as a means by which man can imaginatively preserve some of his possibilities. Since life is a constant reaching beyond itself, actualizing one out of many possible "I's" in our search for happiness, the unelected possibilities all would be lost if some were not saved through artistic actualization.[16]

Most of the literary criticism Marías has written deals with the novel, although he has treated briefly poetry, drama, the essay, and, as we shall see in the next section, the movies. He considers the novel to be the major genre of literary expression of our times since narration portrays the temporality intrinsic to human life. In this way a novel speaks to the private, intimate life of a person. If it failed to do so, it would be intolerable to read. When it succeeds, it offers the reader a vicarious experience of life, an imaginative preparation or rehearsal for actual living.[17] Through novels we are confronted with a multitude of possible experiences that we would otherwise not have, fabulously enriching our lives. In no way is the reading of an authentic novel a waste of time. On the contrary, one gains time, at least in the sense that time, often hundreds of years of possible lives, is abbreviated and condensed in the novel, as well as in the play and motion picture. Young people, and the not-so-young, can fictitiously experience some of what, in earlier times, was known only by the very old. All of us can confront death imaginatively.

In evaluating a novel the critic must ascertain if the double significance of an authentic novel is present: a product of its culture and a possibility of life in that culture. This is seen in the verisimilitude of the novel defined as "circumstantialized narration," in judging whether life as portrayed in the novel is a legitimate possibility.[18] Those novels that transgress this criterion are almost always based on a philosophical error concerning human life. It is not a matter of the novel as a mirror of the real world, but a retention of the vital life of human reality. An author succeeds in giving his fictitious characters and their novelistic circumstances a convincing illusion of reality, a degree of verisimilitude, only when he adopts a perspective that is consistent with itself. Just as a child who is playing a game whose rules are capriciously changed gives up in disgust, so the reader of a novel whose perspective is unfaithful to itself discards the work in frustration.[19]

Closely related to the criterion of verisimilitude is that of the opacity of human life. Unlike an abstract object that is totally transparent to our intelligence, since we created it, but somewhat like a physical object, human life is opaque.[20] All our probing of our own "interiority," to say nothing of that of others, does not dispel a certain amount of mystery. Fictitious personages are not quite as opaque as in real life, having a relative transparency such that we might call them translucid. This gives them a degree of similarity to real persons, yet prevents the author from falsifying human life, as a determinist might do, by pretending he knows all that will happen. Only God has a total apprehension of life, that of man being always partial, involving some degree of opacity.

Poetry is examined by Marías mainly in connection with his study of Unamuno. He concludes that poetic creation is dependent more on a poet's innate feelings and inspirations than on his life's experiences, as in the case of the novel. As a result poets create earlier in life (Unamuno being an exception). They also survive more personally in their creations because the reader can experience analogously the same emotions. This is important in dealing with love as seen in lyric poetry, which has always been considered the imaginative recreation of this form of installation. The literary "style" of love, in turn, has become a decisive factor in real love, for life receives an "emotional coloration" from poetry. Far from being simply entertaining, poetry is necessary in order to live, a sort of dose of "subtle lyrical vitamins."[21] The poet can resort to pure metaphors that barely brush reality, not revealing it as much as attempting to provoke it through rhythm by some sort of spiritual "contagion" so that the reader is carried into the original situation of the poet. Examples of this abound in Unamuno's poetry in his attempt to prelive death. As is proper to poetry, Unamuno is not *saying* anything about death, not even mentioning it by name, but creating the atmosphere of its coming—in a moment unknown to each of us.

The criticism of drama presented by Marías is primarily from the perspective of the viewer, what one can derive from a play. Unlike the novelist and, especially, the poet, the dramatist is only one factor in his art form. Others are the stage, the scenery, the actors, and the audience, all of which are essential. "I believe the most important aspect of the theater, that is, the most distinctive thing about it, which differentiates that form of imaginative representation of human life from all others, is the theater chair. The theater spectator, in effect, is seated; the seat signifies an immobility, and as such a singular point of view, the imposition of a fixed and permanent perspective."[22] In this it differs from the novel, which permits a greater freedom of imaginative wanderings, although the theater has its own type of freedom consisting in the fact that the stage setting does not necessitate everything being said explicitly. The central nucleus of a drama is the audience, which complements the actors to give a sort of double "spectacle," wherein members of the audience are as conscious of each other as of the actors.[23]

As a critic Marías disapproves of obscurity and the cryptic and values clarity and precision. A personal style, he insists, can be created only through writing. It involves more than merely having the urge to write. Talent, self-discipline, and mastery of language are the prerequisites. A man's literary style is a manifestation of his life-style, expressing him even as does his face. It is based, above all, on his inherited language, even as his face is based on biological heredity.[24] If a writer does not discover an adequate style in his historical situation, he must try to invent one. Few are capable of such a new creation, settling for a personalized version of the prevailing style. Style must not be overdone, never acting as an impediment to what is being presented. Otherwise the work will lack what Marías calls "page quality" (*calidad de página*), that aesthetic radiance which provokes a shudder of enjoyment.[25] Such pages are the author speaking in his own voice, revealing his own self, rather than repeating what is in vogue.

VI   *Movies as an Art Form*

As we saw, the historical constitution of human life has been discovered by the twentieth century as by no other. Writers sensitive to the fugacity of life, its fleeting character of rushing into the future, gave to their various forms of contemporary literature a cinematographic quality even before the movies became as widespread as they are. "It is not by chance that movies are an art form of the twentieth century precisely because our age has come to have a cinematographic idea of life: not as a static reality, a thing or an organism, but as something that happens, a drama, a plan which fulfils itself in a world."[26] As such the movies are the latest form of art as the "image" of human life.

From earliest times, as seen in the caves of Altamira, man has created images of human life, even when they were seemingly superfluous. What can be said of the human race, that images give pleasure, can be said of the history of individuals, for children like pictures and, above all, stories. From this has been born all literature, including the forms of movie, radio, and television dramas. That man would seek to complicate his life with duplications or images seems strange until we realize there is no strict separation between the real and the imaginary. The very constitution of our lives makes it necessary to project imaginatively into the future. Where, for example, is the seven o'clock of our appointment when we make it five hours before it occurs? I have no choice but to imagine it, to anticipate it.

The movies, as "a finger that signals," mix the imaginative and the real in a strange way. By means of the lens of the camera we, who are seated in a stationary place in a darkened motion picture house, move along from thing to thing seeing physical objects from different perspectives but apprehending more than the physical— grasping the meanings of situations. Not only are we entertained, but we are stupefied. The movies are a form of drugs, a kind of magic show of "presences" in which still pictures are seen and, then, not seen (*visto y no visto*), that make co-living in our times more effective. Drugs have always had, from the most remotely prehistorical times, a decisive function in human life. To say that a drug might be dangerous proves nothing, because everything in the world, without exception, can be dangerous. "Possibly, the function of movies as a form of stupefaction is more important than its function as art. . . . The movies as art are very important, but there are things more important than art."[27]

Marías's series of movie reviews, which he has been writing regularly for approximately twenty years, constitutes what he has called a cinematographic anthropology. Read separately they are more like the usual well-written review, but when read as a series, and in the context of his analytical and empirical theories of human life, they appear as further elaborations of specific aspects of human life. This is why he can say, when writing about "La lengua y el temple de la vida" [Language and the Temper of Life], in conjunction with the linguistic and social transformation of Eliza Doolittle by Professor Henry Higgins in *My Fair Lady*, that:

An old idea of mine is that the motion picture is a new form of anthropology, or "knowledge of man" if you wish, of the analysis of human reality. That is precisely because the movies try out perspectives inaccessible to the other forms of thought—the motion picture is *also* an original form of thought, and for this reason a special training is needed to understand it—and consequently it reaches unknown facets of reality. . . .[28]

In many senses the knowledge of man presented by the movies has acted as potentially liberating. Thanks to the movies men know what is going on throughout the world, and it has become increasingly difficult to fool them, to convince them that their particular human condition, including the economic, is simply the human condition itself. Motion pictures have dilated the horizons of twentieth-century man by bringing parts of the world within his sight so that he is not confined, as were his ancestors, to his immediate vicinity. They have also opened his eyes to the seemingly minute and insignificant elements surrounding us, those that were never noticed previously or that had been forgotten. Thanks to the movies men notice such details as rain falling on a windowpane, an old man cleaning his glasses, a white wall almost musically vibrating in the sunlight, one step of a staircase, the inside workings of an automobile, the tension of waiting, etc. Above all, motion pictures have forced the cultured man to abandon his abstract notions of living. Love ceases to be a word and is made visible in eyes, gestures, voices, and kisses. Fatigue is the specific figure of a child sleeping in a bed, how one lets his arm fall to his side after working. War is no longer speeches and news bulletins but mud, insomnia, laughter, the happiness of receiving a letter, an amputated hand that never returns, an explosion that announces the inevitable.

Unfortunately, because movies are an entertaining divertissement, the art form is not taken as seriously as it should be. When one leaves a movie, instead of leaving the imaginative for the real, what is happening is that one is passing from the concrete to the abstract. "If the men of our time truly would gather what they learn in the movies, they would see the future with more confidence. What I fear is that after traveling the stirring, intimate corners of the world, they will forget them once back on the street, in order to attend solely to the commonplaces of life."[29]

CHAPTER 7

Evaluations

I *Style and Method: Writer of Theory*

One must attempt, if one wishes to understand a philosophy, to place oneself within it, in such a way that in expounding it, it seems to us that it is justified. There is no need—and it would be a grave error—to try to show the deficiency or falsity of a position without first trying to understand it. One must make the attempt to justify it, to present it from the inside, not in order that one later might go outside it and refute it—a repulsive word if ever there was one—but rather in order to follow within it and attempt to take it seriously and think it through to its basis, to see if it really takes us somewhere or if we trip over some difficulty which obliges us to go beyond it.[1]

THESE words were part of a lecture that was devoted primarily to the role of atheism in Sartre's existentialism. It is what Marías, a believer, attempted to do in regard to Sartre's position, and it is what we have tried to accomplish in respect to Marías's thought. Before proceeding to evaluate some of the key aspects of his contribution, we shall turn our attention to Marías's style in presenting his thoughts.

As we pointed out earlier, Marías contends that a man's literary style is a manifestation of his life-style, expressing him and his aspirations even as does his face.[2] What Marías's style reveals is the synthesis of his disciplined method of ratio-vitalism and his sensitivity to the most important question that can be asked concerning one's self; "What is to become of me?" The method Marías first heard from his mentor Ortega, and in rethinking and applying it he saw for himself its validity. The question—well, that is more difficult to speak of. Certainly he saw it expressed after a fashion, and quite dramatically, in Unamuno. But, so had Ortega. Yet, Ortega never asked himself the question from the depths of his own person. The particular sensitivity that characterizes Marías's response to Unamuno no doubt comes from the fact that Marías had already asked

121

himself the question posed by Unamuno. Perhaps the position of his first professor of philosophy at the University of Madrid, Zubiri, convinced Marías that religion is not incompatible with philosophy, that God does enter philosophy in some way—in our search for our ultimate destiny.

In his treatment of literary style Marías informs us that clarity and precision are to be valued above all else. In his own writing this is quite manifest, as he attempts to avoid the obscure and confused. Time and again the word "clarity" is seen in the words of those reviewing his works. José Angeles observes: "The elegance and fluidity of the phrasing are but the clarity of ideas and the coherence of thought. It is important to notice that the quality of Marías's prose is intrinsic, essential and not superimposed, in his essays."[3] James H. Abbott says: "The author's clear style and explanation help the reader see each idea as it is born and follow its development to a logical conclusion." Again, ". . . [his] straightforward approach is evident throughout . . . in the lucid style with clear explanations which put complicated concepts within the reach of the layman."[4] Francisco Ruiz Ramón maintains that Marías's style shows us his thought coming alive through words, due to a precision that is spontaneously natural.[5] Hans Beerman writes: "The incisive but melodious style conveys to us the tremendous intellectual versatility Marías commands. . . ."[6]

The most extensive treatment of style by Marías is in connection with his treatment of Ortega's style. Many of his observations concerning his mentor likewise apply to him. This is not to say that he imitated Ortega, but that both considered clarity to be the courtesy an author owes his readers. Both realized that the point of departure of a literary style is the various modes in which a writer is installed in life, beginning with language itself, which is already a certain style. They seem to have been of the same accord that style is not secondary or irrelevant for a philosopher. "Style is the substratum, and to that extent intrinsic, of all philosophic doctrine, and at the same time the standard which permits us to measure the degree of authenticity of its realization."[7] Each philosophy assumes a style through which the background life-pattern and linguistic interpretation of reality are manifest. Thus understood, style is the most adequate expression of the concrete situation of a writer. Both writers are given to metaphors and the dramatization of concepts so that they can express life as it is.

Marías found an example of the style that suited him in that of his mentor. It was Ortega whom he must have had in mind when he spoke of the personal creation of a style where none existed, rather than a personal modification of an existing style, as in the case of himself. Such a new style is the supreme gift of a very few writers to their fellow authors. The new style and the new modification of an existing style do not come cheaply or freely, since the act of creation is painful, even if also delightful. Styles are forged in authenticity and discipline.[8]

The union of a disciplined style and a disciplined philosophic method has given Marías the ability to cut in a clear and orderly manner across an enormous amount of experience and knowledge to give his readers the essentials and discard the trivialities of any topic. This is the ability of a gifted and extraordinary author. In this we agree with Beejee Smith.[9] Marías has suited his style to the various genres he has used: newspaper articles, essays, reviews of books and movies, and "novelistic" philosophy books. Although the latter is his most distinctive contribution (as we shall discuss presently), he has earned a lasting place for himself in Spanish literature as an essayist.[10] More often than not, he is referred to simply as an essayist and philosopher. Like Ortega before him, his aesthetic turn of a phrase has brought a philosophic point home to many readers who might otherwise have missed it.

In our estimation, Marías's contribution to literary genres may be his "novelistic" presentation of philosophy, to which we now turn for a closer look. In the essay on "Los géneros literarios en filosofía" [Literary Genres in Philosophy], in which Marías stated that Ortega never wrote a philosophy *book*, he pointed out ". . . that the first *book*, in the strict sense of the term, of philosophy that I wrote . . . was an *Introduction to Philosophy*."[11] Since Marías does not recognize the works of any other philosopher, regardless of how original his contribution and excellent his presentation, as constituting a *book* of philosophy, our conclusion must be that Marías thinks he has written the first such *book*. We shall examine the basis for this implied claim.

As presented in Marías's *History of Philosophy*, all key past philosophical roads lead to Ortega. He built upon his immediate predecessors' discovery of human life, as a reality irreducible to the physical, and offered his vital reason as the instrument to apprehend it philosophically. The result was a renewal of metaphysics and of philosophy. This is, of course, quite a claim but, as any careful examination will show, each philosopher must make much the same claim, either for himself or his mentor. There is no doubt in our mind that Marías has always written with the unshakable conviction that Ortega set philosophy back on its path, and that he himself has faithfully tried to continue and advance Ortega's endeavor. (As stated in our preface, it would require an entire book to examine this claim, and so we have granted Marías his conviction.)

We have seen Marías make his case for the dramatic structure of human life, and for the necessity that philosophic theory be also dramatic in order to account for this. It seems to us that it follows, as Marías maintains, that the literary genre in which "philosophy as dramatic theory" is expressed must also be dramatic.[12] It is not that the philosophy book must be a drama; it is that such a book must *also* have something of the drama about it. In this view a *book* devoted to philosophy must be as rigorously systematic as human life itself, with each of its themes coimplicating the others until the structure of life is uncovered. Problems cannot be simply formulated; they must be arrived at. That is, the author of a book worthy of the name "philosophy" must take the necessary literary steps in order to bring his readers to the point of seeing these problems for themselves.

Has Marías accomplished this? In our estimation, yes—and definitely better than most. The main reason is that he is conscious that the problem of literary genres has a wider sense than it has been considered by those few professional philosophers who have given it thought. Current preoccupation with the problem seems to be limited to producing a better textbook. In the United States the activity surrounding writing a better textbook has been quite furious during the last decade, because students expect something more "relevant" than that with which their predecessors were satisfied, and professors find it more difficult to interest students in philosophy. Some innovative and pedagogically sound books have been the result.

However, the university classroom does not seem to be the aim of Marías. He appears to be directing his works to the general educated public, even his *books* of philosophy. He considers these books to be his *Introduction to Philosophy, The Structure of Society,* and *Ortega: Circumstance and Vocation,* to which he surely would now add *Metaphysical Anthropology.* In our judgment only two definitely belong on the list, the first and the last, with his study of society a possible third. His study of Ortega is incomplete and, so, does not present the entire "dramatic" structure or plot of that philosopher's life and thought.

It may be that there is no way to settle Marías's claim that his works are *the* first books of philosophy *unless* one is convinced that Marías's notion of philosophy *and* his philosophical contribution either *are* or *are not* the *most adequate* available. If the former, the answer is clearly yes; and one adopts Marías as his mentor and starting point in future philosophizing, even as Marías adopted Ortega. If the latter is the case, one already has discovered another mentor, or he himself has personally formulated the basic principles of his own philosophy. If one is in the position of admiring Marías's development of what he understands to be Ortega's original insights and of contributing much of his own that is original, as we are, then *to this degree* only can it be acknowledged that Marías has written philosophy *books*. If one also admires and agrees with contributions by others, as is the case with this writer, then Marías's claim is too exclusive. A philosophy "text" need be as *explicitly* dramatic in structure as are the books by Marías that we mentioned *only* if it is read without the assistance of a professional philosopher. If the "text" is to be transformed into a textbook by a professional philosopher, through classroom lectures and discussions, it is sufficient that it be *implicitly* dramatic in structure, as we believe are many other "texts" by philosophers other than Marías.

All of Marías's writings on philosophy clearly manifest that he has situated himself firmly in the camp of those who insist that philosophy be studied through its history, in contrast to those who see its history as irrelevant to philosophy. The controversy concerning the relation of philosophy to its own history, how philosophy uses its past, is one of the most difficult and complex problems in contemporary philosophy. However, the main lines of the controversy are not as clear as at first meets the eye, and Marías's position is a case in point. On the one hand, he asserts that an appeal to the history of philosophy in trying to understand philosophy is "as legitimate as it is indispensable," and all philosophizing includes the entire history of philosophy. On the other hand, he emphasizes the need to philosophize "in view of things." We believe that a clarification of his seemingly conflicting statements will go a long way in focusing on the key issues in the controversy of philosophy versus the history of philosophy.

At the center of the controversy is the metaphysical problem of the nature of human life. Unless the development of a human is acknowledged to be in history, that is, unless the very being of the human being is seen to be essentially historical, the controversy is hopelessly muddled. Those contemporary philosophical movements that disdain engaging in metaphysics as "nonsense" are immediately crippled in their ability to engage in mutually beneficial dialogue. It is mainly this group that tends to see philosophy as having no use for its history.

We interpret Marías to mean that it is not a matter of *either* paying heed to the *words* of our philosophic forebears, *or* viewing *things* entirely on our own. The two must be done successively and, then, simultaneously, as Marías did in regard to Ortega. Ever since "abstract" knowledge was misunderstood as an intellectual perspective that could ignore experience, even if it had originated in things, we have been open to the temptation of opting for words over things. Marías's position attempts to reconcile the two and, in our estimation, he presents a most convincing case for the need to keep one eye on the words of our predecessors in philosophizing, and the other on things in our circumstances. In this manner each of us can verify for himself the discoveries of the giants in philosophy through an appeal to things, and experience the same vital satisfaction of philosophy assisting us in our endeavor to live authentically in our specific historical circumstances.[13]

II   *On the Frontiers of Philosophical Anthropology*

By far Marías's most original and profound contribution to philosophic theory is his *Metaphysical Anthropology*. We would venture to say that if it were the *only* work he had written, it would insure him of a highly deserved reputation as a thinker with insight and foresight. As we pointed out in chapter 3, Marías himself acknowledges that the theme, of a kind of reality neither essential nor accidental, is not completely new.[14] But, his development of it is unique—as dynamic, vectorlike forms of installation rooted in the prerequisites of human life and further concretized in the historical characteristics of individual humans. In our estimation, especially striking in this context are his contentions that human life need not have taken exactly the form it has on earth, that sexuateness is disjunctive, and that language is a binding observance that *is* our fundamental interpretation of reality (rather than merely a *means* to such an interpretation). We shall turn our attention to these issues, concluding with a word about the fruitfulness for psychology of Marías's theory of person.

There is no doubt the lunar landing on 20 July 1969 had a profound impression on Marías as he was working on the manuscript of *Metaphysical Anthropology*. In chapter 13, on "Worldhood," he pointed out: "Until now, 'man' has been the slave of the terrestrial globe; in principle—though only in principle—he no longer is, and this is enough to have changed his world structure."[15] Marías sees man's journey to the moon as the first step in interplanetary exploration.

If man, upon reaching another planet does not find any life or finds only "biological" life—plants and animals—he will undoubtedly feel cheated; obviously, he desired or hoped to find "men"; but if he finds "men," I fear that he likewise will feel defrauded, thinking that it was not necessary to travel such a long journey just for this. What, then, does he look forward to and hope for? For me there is no doubt: "life"—understood as biographical life, personal life—but with another empirical structure. That is, what we call "human life"—because we have experience of no other form—but not "men."[16]

As far as we know, Marías is the only well-known philosopher to have raised the possibility of human life on other planets, let alone to suggest that life might have a different empirical structure there. The ignorance or neglect of the dimension Marías calls the empirical structure of human life by philosophers renders it highly unlikely that such a possibility is even conceivable in their philosophical anthropologies. This is the major area, in our estimation, in which Marías is truly on the frontiers of philosophical anthropology, and could lead the way to future philosophical theorizing. Unfortunately, not even those few philosophers who are interested in extraterrestrial intelligence seem to be acquainted with Marías's contribution.[17] An excellent, but largely neglected, area for immediate philosophical participation in such theorizing is science fiction. As Ray Bradbury points out, it is through science fiction that we in the present can create possible futures.[18] In this connection it is encouraging to see that a session was devoted to "Philosophy and Science Fiction" at the recent annual conference of the Science Fiction Research Association, and that another dealt with "Science Fiction as Philosophical Literature: Topics in Metaphysics and Epistemology" at the convention of the Popular Culture Association.[19]

Two issues in Marías's philosophical anthropology must be clarified further if serious errors are not to result when speaking of the absolutely prerequisite elements for human life. The first deals with whether corporeality is essential to human life. In both his essay on "Psychiatry from the Point of View of Philosophy" (1952) and his study on *Woman in the Twentieth Century* (1980), Marías states explicitly that it is, but, of course, understood as not necessarily in the form it has taken on earth. There is a passage in *Metaphysical Anthropology* (1970), however, that appears to contradict this assertion. He writes: "[In] principle human life is 'conceivable' in an incorporeal manner (on the condition that this does not signify a merely negative concept, that is, with the exigency of positively thinking of another form of reality as 'homologous' to corporeality)."[20] The issue is dropped at this point. The implication is that human life as incorporeal must not be thought of as being *deprived* of a body, as a person surviving in an "afterlife" might be said to live. (Language, restricted as it is to referring to sense objects, can point out such a form of life only in a negative manner, since "incorporeality" means "noncorporeal.") Incorporeal humans never would have had bodies but, presumably, would have a form of reality "homologous" to corporeality in order that they might be "in" some world or another. After much reflection, we confess that we still cannot understand what Marías had in mind in this passage. We interpret "homologous" to involve some sort of reality that, at least, functions in a manner similar to the human body of "man." We cannot "conceive" of it other than as corporeal. Unless this passage is developed further by Marías, it appears to be irreconcilable with his other statements. We cannot refrain from wondering whether an extraphilosophical factor is operative here, perhaps a religious one, for Marías appears to mean something other than corporeality in a different manifestation than that on earth.

The second issue that must be clarified is more serious, since it can lead to potentially dangerous social relationships. It can be seen in one form in Aristotle, and was used by anti-Indian forces among the early Spaniards to justify their maltreatment of the natives of the Americas. It affirms that human life exists in forms more or less perfect. It seems to us that Ortega's principle, accepted by Marías, that everything human admits of degrees,[21] is open to misunderstanding, especially by those interpreters of Ortega who (erroneously) see his *Revolt of the Masses* as an elitist theory based on an exaltation of a natural aristocracy and a disdain for the less gifted masses. In the context of the metaphysical discovery that human life is in the making, Ortega's principle is understandable. But, unless *what it does not mean* in the sociopolitical area is made explicit, the principle is an obstacle to the very liberal attitude that Ortega and Marías shared, especially in regard to the contemporary civil rights movement in all its forms.

Marías's treatment of the disjunctive reciprocity of the sexes stands out as a significant contribution to philosophy, especially since the sexuate condition, along with corporeality or embodiment as its ground, was strikingly neglected in philosophy until contemporary times. While the modern definition of "man" as a thinking thing virtually excluded a serious consideration of the sexuate condition, the classical and medieval acceptance of "man" as a rational animal certainly implied sexuality, even if little effort was made to philosophize about it. The result was either the complete ignoring of this condition or the implication that it is a secondary, or accidental, attribute rather than a property (consequences probably strengthened by prevailing religious convictions). Even the contemporary discussion is not very widespread, but what has been undertaken is a hopeful commencement. In this respect Marías's theory of the sexuate condition as disjunctive, based as it is on the distinction between sexuality and the sexuate, is most promising as an instrument for future discussions. The philosophers to whom Marías's contribution should be of the greatest interest are those presently theorizing about woman.

Marías is entirely correct in observing that men rarely think, in any intellectual sense, about women, this being evident in the history of philosophy, exclusively a male preserve in a male-centered and largely sexually segregated culture, until the most recent times. Given this situation, it is understandable, even if unfortunate, that contemporary theoretical preoccupation with woman has come to be of interest primarily to female philosophers, who frequently must argue that the theme is a legitimate one for philosophy.

In regard to Marías's contribution to the theme of woman, of course as part and parcel of the sexuate condition as disjunctive, this historical fact of woman's preoccupation with woman as a philosophical theme is a two-edged sword. On the one hand, as Maryellen MacGuigan has correctly stated, Marías has pointed out the "problem" of woman most accurately, recognizing it explicitly as a problem of human life and not as one located peculiarly in woman.[22] Marías's contribution goes a long way in providing a more satisfactory frame of reference for future discussions, since it prevents the philosophical from being lost in solely feminist issues. On the other hand, there is the distinct possibility that Marías either will be dismissed before sufficient consideration or will be misunderstood because of his manner of presentation and/or omissions. Even MacGuigan's clearly sympathetic reading of Marías concludes that, although he defines the sexuate relationship as one of reciprocal reference, ". . . he also defines woman relatively to man in a one-sided way."[23]

After much reflection, we must concur with her statement, at least insofar as the reciprocity proposed by Marías is not clearly carried through in *Metaphysical Anthropology*. It appears, from certain of his statements, as though woman is perceived as related to man in a more intrinsic manner than man is said to be related to woman. The damaging psychological impact of statements, such as "[there] is nothing needier or more uncertain than a woman alone . . . ,"[24] in regard to the insecurity of human life, which *both* man and woman *alike* are supposed to share as human, offset the more numerous ones in which the relationship between the sexes is unequivocally reciprocal. In certain instances we look in vain for a reciprocal treatment of the complementary sex that insures what Marías maintains, that man and woman be kept "on the same level" to insure the fullness of their encounter. Multiple readings of such passages, with the most sympathetic of attitudes to avoid taking a statement out of context, has convinced us that Marías's presentation is open to misinterpretation by the very philosophers who have the most to benefit from his treatment. The issue is extremely important from the perspective of the history of philosophy, for a philosopher's contribution, in large part, stems from the willingness of those much less creative than he to spend valuable time studying him in an effort to understand his position so as to adopt it as their starting point in further considerations of the theme—acknowledging him as their source.

It must be pointed out explicitly that Marías's treatment of the anthropological fact of the sexuate condition is metaphysical rather than sociopolitical, otherwise he will be criticized for what he was not even attempting to do. His statement calling the equality of the sexes one of the most dangerously stupid errors which we could possibly make would be in contradiction with his affirmation of the liberal attitude if he were treating the theme politically. The anthropological balance between the sexes, made up of inequality and tension, for which he calls, seemingly would demand an equality in the legal sense in civil society. The fundamental belief of the liberal tradition in the creation of all "men" as equal deals with the basic civil liberties, without which the fulfillment of human life in any of its forms would be impossible. Any effort to grant a privileged special status to one sex, basing it on special anthropological status, is bound to lessen the authenticity of both sexes, since each only becomes human, as Marías agrees, in relation to the other.

The possible misunderstandings concerning Marías's philosophy of woman in *Metaphysical Anthropology* are offset, we believe, by his elaboration of the same theme in the later treatment entitled *Woman in the Twentieth Century*. There it is quite clear that Marías is calling for the dropping of those binding observances that impede women entering the various professions, as a result of which the world will finally see a feminine realization of those human possibilities that have hitherto been expressed only in a masculine version. He rejoices that he has been born in a century in which such is becoming possible, so that he can co-live with women who are in possession of their integral human condition.[25]

The third contention of Marías that is particularly striking to us is his theory of language. There are three aspects that comprise the theory. The first is Marías's position that language embodies the primary interpretation of reality. The others are that reality is constitutively in need of interpretation to be reality, and that language is a binding observance, the primary means by which we are socialized. As far as we can determine, none of these three elements is original with Marías, having originated with Ortega and others. What is original, we think, is the combination of the three to produce a rather unique, and philosophically promising, theory. Marías's position holds that interpretability is part and parcel of the metaphysical structure of reality, giving rise to interpretations in man's need to know what reality (human life) is in order to live. This interpretation, in its primary or fundamental form, is language—really languages, since various tongues have arisen. Language is not a neutral means by which we express and communicate our interpretations, but *is* the interpretation. Thus, we cannot ignore language in seeking the metaphysical structure of reality. This much the various language philosophies have been maintaining or implying in contemporary times, but without recognizing the interpretability of the real. But there is more. As a binding observance, language is seen to be forced on us at an early and impressionable age, directing and facilitating, as well as limiting, our thinking. Only rigorous reflection, seldom undertaken, can exhibit its restrictive nature, so that most people are not conscious of being completely bound. In our estimation, this is one of the most potentially fruitful areas for discussion and development in Marías's entire position, bringing in as it does linguistic philosophy and sociology, and opening up the possibility of an exchange with language philosophy, the most powerfully influential movement in English-language philosophy in our time. Of particular interest in this context should be Marías's notion of negative binding observances (*solencias*), and their effect on the social activity of women, who have had to make their way in "a man's world."[26]

The theory of human life developed by Marías has had its greatest impact, thus far, on psychology. Marías's interest in the field is such that he is a member of the Spanish Psychological Society. To date, to our knowledge, no formal treatment has appeared in print, but it may be only a matter of time. Conspicuous among the group of psychologists whom he has influenced is José Luis Pinillos—currently teaching psychology at the University of Madrid—who has known Marías since approximately 1948. Pinillos considers that he owes Marías a professional debt. He finds that the kind of psychology one develops depends to a great extent on one's philosophy of man. In this regard Pinillos has said that the theories of vital reason and of the empirical structure of human life of Ortega and Marías have constituted ". . . a philosophic support of the first order, most appropriate for psychology. . . ."[27] Moreover, he reminds his fellow psychologists in Spain that they have no need to import philosophical positions, for Marías's theories are consistent with the peculiarities of Hispanic culture.

In the estimation of Mario Parajón, the psychiatric resonance of Marías's theory of human life is especially significant, since he proposes a study of biographical abnormalities, "bioatry." The emphasis here would not be on the "resources" with which a person is endowed, nor on his childhood traumas, but on what may be said to be biographically abnormal, on those actions in which a person engages in order to avoid facing the tasks which have been placed on him as a person.[28] Joseph Rubin, a child psychologist, sees Marías's philosophy as especially relevant to person-oriented professionals. Unlike behaviorism and positivism, Marías's approach keeps alive the metaphorical and philological in the apprehension of life, thus containing ". . . a subtle and challenging system of ideas with which to examine language, happiness, freedom, becoming, and the vital differentiation between the masculine and feminine person."[29]

III   *Philosopher in the Market Place*

Above all, Marías has not been the victim of agoraphobia, the fear of the public. Unlike the overwhelming majority of contemporary philosophers, he has not been an "ivory tower" thinker, his outgoing situation necessitated by the fact that he could not hold an official position in a university in his own country. His work has been more in the public eye, something that seems to be compatible with his outgoing personality, including his love of traveling to meet new societies and people. In this section we shall examine the method he employed in obtaining his reflections, especially on the United States, and his social attitude of liberalism.

The question of the validity of Marías's travel reflections must be raised. Their validity depends on two factors: the method employed to attain the reflections, and the "light" the reflections throw on the region or country which elicited them. Quite early in his career Marías characterized his method of writing about countries as constituted by impressionism and analysis. As we saw, he maintains that impressionism saves his reflections from becoming abstractions, "fleshless speculations," while analysis prevents them from being deceptive or superficial.

All knowledge, as we understand it, must include what we shall call the subjective and objective poles. That is, a statement that purports to declare anything about a state of existential affairs must be grounded in the knower (subject) and the known (object). Knowledge is, in this view, the reciprocal interaction of these two poles. Does Marías's method meet these requirements of knowledge? We think so. As we see it, the initial observation—upon which all knowledge directly or indirectly depends—puts the knower in touch with the *object*. Unless the observation is grounded in, or interpreted by, theories that arose from previous experience of some kind, they remain physical reactions (much like what occurs in photographic reproductions, electronic recording, and computer information depositing and retrieval). This placing of sense data within the biographical context of the *subject* manifests the opposite pole.

However, the poles must also be reversed. The initial observation, which is the objective pole, becomes the subjective one to the degree to which the subject feels a need to know and deliberately open himself to his circumstances. As a result, the observation is an impression. This is exactly what we understand by Marías's method of impressionism. Marías felt he had to open himself to the countries and regions to which he traveled in order to become himself through fulfilling his vocation. If this were all he would have done, his impressions would have been isolated or abstract speculation, simply revealing his idiosyncrasies. It is the grounding of the isolated impressions within their proper context that introduces the objective pole, since reality itself is interconnected, and makes his reflections contributions toward understanding society. This is the role of the method of analysis, the referring of everything to the "whole," as Marías stated it. Eventually he will call this "whole" or proper context the social structure. It is by connecting our particular experiences with the social structures from which they emerge that we are able to detect the pattern of life of a given national or regional society.

Parallel to the theoretical principles of impressionism and analysis that constitute his method, the grounding of details in their totality, Marías lists another group which he calls "moral" principles. The cardinal one here is considered to be the recognition that "it is never possible to know deeply and completely any country save one's own."[30] This is a respect for the "secret" of each country, each people. A foreign country gradually begins to be less foreign, however, "by dint of time, love, and intelligence."[31] One can get to know a people relatively well, though less quickly than he can come to know another person. It simply takes time, and involves co-living, with the risk of failure always present. Much of the observation required is based on the "reading of faces" whose gestures reveal the hidden binding observances of their respective societies. It also takes love, the enthusiastic willingness to go forth and truly meet the people in their own circumstantial context. Closed-mindedness and prejudice, in the literal sense of prejudgment of what will be found, are obstacles. The intelligence involved is the need of the theoretical principles already spoken of, otherwise one's impressions are isolated and deceptive. For anyone prepared and willing to live by these dual principles the result is ". . . one of the deepest emotions, one of the greatest delights man can enjoy, an unexpected extension of his life and personality, something vaguely similar to the loving conquest of a woman, equally problematic, difficult, and uncertain."[32] A foreign traveler who has written about a country without having lived among its people by these principles carried his book under his arm when he arrived, the case, Marías thinks, with most books about the United States.[33]

The American response to Marías's reflections on their country has been very positive. Most agree that he consciously tried to avoid the usual stereotypes that have distorted the vision of other commentators. As a result, Americans can learn much about themselves, as we are sure their author learned much about himself and his own people by constantly contrasting the two cultures. Without being an apologist for the United States, and never ceasing to be an "arch-European," Marías found the form of life he experienced from the "inside" to be "endearing." That it is necessary to experience any country, any people, in this manner is a paramount requisite of his social theory. As Marías states in *The Structure of Society*, binding observances are unintelligible if understood from the outside, for they lack their proper context wherein each acts in concert with the others—reinforcing, accompanying, and counterbalancing each other. This is not the epistemological claim that only those who are part of a particular group can know it, what the American sociologist Robert Merton refers to as the "Doctrine of the Insider" in his introduction to the English translation of the book.[34] It is the call for a "hermeneutical transmigration to the situation in question," of imaginatively placing oneself in the world being examined—as a traveler rather than as a tourist—so that one may assume vicariously what is (or could have been, if a past society is being studied, recreating the life of one of its inhabitants). In this manner the true-to-life pressures of the general binding observances that constitute the society, including earning a living, having and running a househhold, making one's own purchases, and associating with neighbors, can be lived and felt.[35]

As Michael Aaron Rockland pointed out in his introduction to the English translation of the combined volumes of Marías's essays on the United States, Marías did this quite well, to the point of being blinded—as were most Americans themselves—to the presence of poverty in the country in the 1950s. His eyes were more open to the presence of a confidence in the times that began to wane in the 1960s, detecting this change of temperament.[36] Marías feels that most of America's problems are of its own making, some being figments of its imagination, even if no less real in their results. However, he still is hopeful for the future of the United States, as especially sensitive to humankind's possibilities, despite the fact that there are "unmistakable signs of infection," "certain dark clouds" on the horizon, and a farfetched notion of happiness.

According to Russell Kirk, "[of] Europeans' recent surveys of American character and society, perhaps only Marías's book may be found truly interesting a century from now."[37] This is due to Marías's "good-natured observations" that hold "so much for the common reader." It is due to his sincere contention that the United States is one of the great creations of history, like Rome or the

Spanish Empire, that deserves to be studied enthusiastically, to his conclusion that the great novelty of the United States is precisely that it is a "new life" with a structure that is unique. "Marías himself is never bored with America" (although he sees boredom insidiously beginning to pervade American life), as is evident in his essays on the most incredible range of topics, including the bureaucracy, spelled with a capital *B*, which he views as a form of "Satanism that seeks to replace God by the temporal organization."[38] Marías's format, of short impressionistic essays, is found to be both provocative and disappointing by Howard T. Young. It is a disappointment because it could have been so much more—". . . a longer and more coherent study of the United States and what it means," an omission that causes the first volume, according to Young, to just miss "being of major importance."[39] Kirk, however, concludes that Marías's two volumes are a success. Even if they are not widely read, they are successful for they show an author who feels no rivalry with the United States and seeks to please no one, not even editors, directors, and critics of the publishing business. Like Tocqueville's *Democracy in America* (which Marías finds still the most timely and intelligently written book on America), Kirk finds Marías's book to be valuable because both are written by authors who were sure of their own identities and could compare clearly their own people with those of their host country.

As William McCann pointed out, Marías ". . . has an eye for the small but significant things that enables him to extract profit and pleasure from prosaic experience."[40] Marías walks the frequently trodden roads without being dulled or dulling, with no malice and shallow impertinence when discussing those aspects of American society he finds distasteful. Probably and inevitably he generalizes on too narrow a range of observations, but "is sure enough of his insights and intuitions to risk being wrong, to make the informed and spirited guess. As a result, we sometimes get interpretations from him as brilliant as Tocqueville's. . . ."[41] Originally directed to his countrymen—as these essays were—"Spanish readers can scarcely be expected to realize how grateful they should be for this lucid, profound commentary on a foreign civilization by a man who brings such wide historical and philosophical perspectives to bear on his theme."[42] At least one Spanish critic, Juan López-Morillas, in reviewing the first volume, declared it to be the most profound, revealing, and just book that has been written by a foreigner on the United States.[43] Certainly from the American perspective we can agree with Durant da Ponte that Marías is an especially keen observer of the United States,[44] with Howard T. Young that his fairness is admirable, not deriding those aspects he finds wanting,[45] and with Robert E. Lott that Marías treats all his topics perspicaciously and intelligently.[46]

The areas of Marías's interpretations that most interest us are American philosophy and academic life, perhaps the topics in which Marías has reason to feel more confident in his judgments. The institution of the university has been captured admirably by Marías, both from the outside as a foreigner and from the inside as one who taught and lectured here extensively, and at a larger number of institutions than most American professors ever visit. He touches on the key elements in an American university: its setting (the campus that often resembles a park); its offerings (the curriculum with an amazing variety of offerings); and its function (the social role of the institution). We shall limit our comments to the last aspect.

It is no easy task, as Marías observes, to answer the question of the role of the university in American society. In general, as with other institutions of learning, it is to educate an individual so as to form a person. This implies, as Marías correctly concludes, a community role in the moral formation of the person that extends beyond the usual home and church. Education, accordingly, involves three things: the knowledge necesary in a given discipline (to enter the professions or other employment), a synthesis of the dominant ideas of the time (mostly through required and elective courses in a variety of fields), and a system of beliefs and norms of behavior (what some universities call "values"). Marías is correct in concluding that "in the United States the latter is the most decisive, and around it all others are arranged."[47]

The imparting of beliefs and ideas must be done critically, an accomplishment that is impossible without the study of philosophy. But, as pointed out by Marías from his perspective of teaching in the Department of Philosophy at Yale in the 1950s, Americans have yet to realize that they *need* what philosophy has to offer, namely, an opportunity to learn who they are in order to become the people they feel they must. When the need is finally realized, he continued, the risk is that there will be no authentic philosophy at hand. Americans will turn to false philosophies, false for their circumstances.[48]

Has this already happened, we might ask? To a limited extent, yes. During the last two decades national and international crises have triggered changes in American co-living. Most have viewed these changes as superficial and temporary, rather than as affecting the very social aims and aspirations of our collective co-living. Some of the latter have turned, especially, to varieties of Marxism that have little to do with conditions in the United States. (The least they could have done was consider the creative "critical" Marxisms of Eastern Europe.)

Advocating an "American" philosophy, as does Marías, is not a contradiction in terms. Philosophy deals with all of reality and all of humankind, such that any position that is devoid of a universality commensurate with humankind is not philosophy. What could be called "American" about philosophy, as what was once "Greek" about it, or may be "Spanish" about Marías's own position, is the consideration of problems in human living connected with the circumstantial situation of life in the United States. A beginning was made, as we see it, by John Dewey during the first half of this century. Like Ortega and Marías, Dewey was not an "ivory tower" thinker. Like them, he sought to take into account actual conditions in his country. Unfortunately, no one has succeeded him in this effort.

The social attitude (*temple*) in Marías's interest in all aspects of co-living, as we have seen, is his liberalism. Marías is sensitive to his social duties, but constantly maintains his right to a private dimension in his life, as might be expected of one whose vocation is philosophy. This means he has "done his best"—as a Spaniard, a European, a Westerner, a man, and a person—in the various political circumstances in which he has found himself. It is little wonder that Marías once said that, if he had a seal, his motto would be "*Por mí que no quede*"—variously translated as "I do my part," "If no one else will, I will," "It won't be my fault if it fails," or "I'll do my best [under the circumstances]."[49]

Marías's liberalism is not embodied in any existing political party in Spain, or, as far as we can ascertain, anywhere else. It is a historico-social orientation that could be shared by many who might disagree on issues sufficiently disparate to warrant separate political organizations. Marías does not seem to have the temperament for partisan politics, for which he has probably been criticized by professional politicians as was Ortega before him. It may be that present-day governments do not offer a person an opportunity to exercise statesmanship, the only manner in which we can imagine Marías's being active in the political arena.

We saw Marías's definition of liberalism as being "enthusiastic or skeptical melancholy," exhibiting as it does a balance between the two poles that have characterized political activity: confidence in reason with disregard of emotions, or emotional reaction undisciplined with reason. As Michael A. Weinstein, professor of political science at Purdue University, has observed, Marías is in the tradition of great liberals such as José Vasconcelos, who defined his temperament as "happy pessimism," and George Santayana, who called our everyday life "normal madness." Weinstein himself has used the term "ruthless compassion" to do the same sort of work.[50] This use of an oxymoron permits, Weinstein states, ". . . the use of irony, distance, individuality, and a certain generosity shot through with strength."[51] We agree with Weinstein when he says that Marías experiences liberalism from within, by which we interpret Weinstein as meaning from the perspective that comes from interior freedom of thought and privacy in one's personal life, that Marías continually emphasized, rather than merely in external democratic institutions.

Two other characteristics of Marías's liberalism may be pointed out. One is what Weinstein calls its negative virtue, based on Marías's observation that liberalism is the political system that has failed the least, enabling us to attain a certain level of tranquillity because we live by a belief that the system has its limits, and will not permit certain things to happen. As Weinstein recalls, this is paramount to Marías's generation, given its political experience with totalitarianism. The other note of Marías's liberalism is that it must be concrete (to avoid the criticism usually levied against it by conservatives and Marxists). That is, no theory, ideology, or party can contain liberalism wholly, because it is rooted in the situation, a situation which is an ongoing part of human life itself.

IV   *Circumstance and Vocation: Spanish Philosopher*

In the words of Marías:

There are two radical ingredients in human life that are not the object of choice. The first is *circumstance;* the second is *vocation.* I have not chosen to be a man, nor Spanish, nor to be born in the twentieth century, nor my family, nor my country; I have not chosen the body and the soul I have; none of these have I chosen; I simply have found myself with them. And neither have I chosen my vocation. . . . A vocation is a voice that summons, that calls me. . . . I have to choose whether or not to follow my vocation, if I am to be faithful or unfaithful to it; I do not choose it, and precisely for this reason it is my vocation, my destiny. I feel myself called to be someone and I freely choose to be faithful or unfaithful to this vocation, in the same way I choose what I am going to do with the endowments that are given me, with my body and my soul and my world.[52]

In this context, it is clear that Marías's circumstance is Spain and his vocation is a writer of philosophy. No doubt he had planned to pursue his doctorate after his first degree was awarded in June of 1936, having a university teaching career in mind. The Civil War and his imprisonment would have seemed like insurmountable obstacles to one of less determination. His first book, *History of Philosophy*, created still another obstacle to his being faithful to his vocation. Utilizing the societal categories Marías adopted, we can see that he had violated two of the strongest binding observances of Spanish society during those years. Above all, that to which one was bound during the post–Civil War years was the social legitimacy of the Franco regime. Marías, with his liberal attitude, simply could not accept this, and paid the price for forty years by remaining ineligible for appointment to a position that required official government approval. If the dictatorial regime had been uniformly totalitarian as well, Marís would not have been able to have anything published in Spain, or his manuscripts sent out of Spain, or to give private lessons. In other words, he would have been forcibly exiled or, worse, kept in prison. As if this binding observance were not sufficiently damaging, Marías violated a second one, one that required that those who teach philosophy in a government-controlled institution be Scholastic in their position. Franco's alliance with the Catholic Church gave churchmen control of education on all levels. The official philosophy of the Catholic Church was (and still is) Scholasticism, with an emphasis on the position of Saint Thomas Aquinas. Marías's explicit adherence to the position of Ortega, as seen in his *History of Philosophy*, placed an additional lock on an already-closed door. Even membership in the official Falange party would not have sufficed to open the door.

Ortega had been considered an agnostic relativist, if not an outright atheist, by Spanish ecclesiastics. Their views never changed, as can be seen by the polemic during Ortega's last years, and especially following his death. The customary expressions of condolence and weak praise for the dead were allowed, even in the party organ *Arriba*, perhaps more for foreign than internal consumption since everyone knew the regime's attitude toward Ortega. The "absolute secularism" of this international figure was pointed out, even if some did excuse his religious insensitivity because of the bad examples of his youth. The archbishop of Toledo, Miranda Vicente, in a speech entitled "What We Have Not Been Told About Ortega," made a distinction between Ortega the man and Ortega's work, maintaining that anyone with his qualifications would not be a fit educator for that day. A pastoral letter appeared in which it was said that atheists and materialists, skeptics and relativists, were unfit to be teachers of Spanish youth. In such an atmosphere Marías, who seemingly put himself forward as the heir of Ortega, could never have been appointed to a teaching position. The Franco regime did not interfere with his election to the Spanish Royal Academy in 1964, but after all, Marías was not militantly anti-Franco, and he had even declared to the foreign press that writers have "freedom of the tongue" in Spain.[53]

That for which the Scholastic philosophers could not forgive Ortega was his ignoring of the "Christian" themes of philosophy, and that for which they seemingly do not forgive Marías is his assertion that Scholasticism, for all its contributions, is a philosophy of the past, not grappling with contemporary problems and thereby maintaining itself at the required height of the times.[54] Marías's assertions concerning immortality must seem like metaphysical agnosticism to their mind,[55] and his discussion of the existence of God must appear as undermining their own position, as well as the church's official teaching that there is "proof" from reason alone that God exists.[56]

Of course, there is no doubt that Marías believes that God exists, or that the contingency of human life points beyond itself. Yet, his metaphysics does not culminate in the "proof" of a Necessary Being as does that of Scholasticism. It evidently hurt Marías to see in print what Jacques Maritain, one of the world's most influential Thomists, had said of his friend, the French existentialist Gabriel Marcel, a convert like Maritain to Catholicism, namely, that only those Catholics are Thomists who are sufficiently intelligent to be such.[57] On the other hand, he had gone against a very powerful binding observance. Not only had he disagreed that all philosophical roads led to Thomas Aquinas and his self-appointed heirs, but he had put Ortega in Aquinas's key position and claimed to be his mentor's heir. To make matters worse, one of his examples of the mass-man mentality was that of a priest speaking out on philosophical matters, as if his key position in directing a religious group gave him authority in all other groups. In a country and time in which clericalism was a binding observance, this could not fall on friendly ears.[58]

Others besides Marías have insisted that Ortega's position is not incompatible with the dogmas of Catholicism. The most notable, in our estimation, is Ciriaco Morón Arroyo, whose monumental study of Ortega's system contains an entire chapter devoted to the matter. He attempts to show that ratio-vitalism can assist us in understanding the theological virtues and the dogmas of the Trinity, the Incarnation, and the Eucharist.[59] Certain contemporary Spanish philosophers are even known as Catholic disciples of Ortega. José Luis Abellán lists Marías among those who belong to the movement of Christian Spiritualism that has its inspiration in Ortega.[60] The unsigned introduction to Marías's *Tres visiones de la vida humana* [Three Visions of Human Life] mentioned him as, above all, being the one who brought to light the hidden religious elements in Ortega's philosophy.[61] Edward Sarmiento devoted a short essay to Marías, whom he calls a Catholic disciple of Ortega, even if an independent one. He writes: "It would be, I am quite sure, a mistake to attribute to Sr. Marías any real disconformity with the mind of the Catholic Church but—and he is not alone in this—he would prefer a new approach to the question of the use to be made of traditional philosophy."[62] According to Marías, a contemporary Catholic philosopher must realize that the new element in our situation today, unlike during the days of Scholasticism, is that we can no longer even assume that the world we live in is Christian. This "ex-Christian" world, however, still manifests the remnants of the faith.

V   An Open-Ended Summation

Our evaluation of Marías's contribution to philosophy must remain open-ended for two reasons. The subject of this book, in his own studies of others, put our reasons in his characteristically succinct and clear manner. First:

Faced with anything whatsoever, we must have its dates of insertion in history, and without them we will not understand it. All that is given is done so in a historical circumstance. . . . In order to understand any human name we must collect the two dates which limit its life, and we must presently anticipate the second date, even though uncertain, in our own lives, substituting for it a question mark.[63]

Without these dates a human life seems incomplete, and we even feel curiously uneasy in regard to our living contemporaries and our very selves, as if we were "deficient" or "imperfect"—for that is what we literally are, imperfect or incomplete in regard to our death as something necessary.[64] Marías, who is still living and very much active as we write this, has before him various possibilities which, depending on those he chooses to actualize, will reflect back over his entire life, modifying its "meaning" to a greater or lesser degree. Marías can choose, for example, to turn his attention to formulating explicitly an "ethics of authenticity." which is the one major area also explicitly absent in the system of his mentor. And, he may complete his monumental study of Ortega's circumstance and vocation, thus throwing more light on the development of his mentor's position, and thereby the genesis and maturation of his own philosophy. Or, Marías may himself be able to say the words that Ortega uttered in 1928: "When I some day write my *Memoirs*, I shall try to do it the way I feel it ought to be done. *Memoirs*, or their substitute the novel, in which we recount our life propose, above all, to save [*salvar*] it, to prevent its absolute volatilization. We want, as a grateful person, to return to life that which it has given us, or what we have uprooted from it, to return it, to return it after having meditated on it and [cognitively] distilled it."[65]

The second reason our evaluation must remain open-ended is that part of Marías's contribution to philosophy, the most distinctive portion, remains largely in the future. Every commentator on his work acknowledges him as the foremost disciple and expositor of Ortega's philosophy. But, they likewise refer to his significant development of that philosophy. Part of what Marías is, is what he *may be*, depending on what happens to his thought in the future in the history of philosophy, as he once mentioned in regard to Unamuno.[66] He will remain on the fringes of professional philosophy, largely studied by those interested in the literature of ideas, unless a special effort is made, by those who consider his contribution penetrating and fruitful for further discussion, to carry his work into the professional arena, into meetings and journals. The same, of course, can be said of those who are professionals in history, sociology, and psychology. As Harold C. Raley observed, Marías, who sees the greatest mission of man to be seeking and telling the truth, despite the fact that in our times man lives "against the truth," gives us a clear and rare vision of truth in his philosophy.[67] What makes Marías's vision rare is that it springs from his "intellectual heroism," in the words of Helio Carpintero, from Marías's conviction to speak out despite his repressive political circumstances.[68] In doing so, as Juan López-Morillas states, Marías has gone a long way in reestablishing faith in the ability of intellectuals to observe our situation clearly so as to assist us in resolving our problems.[69] Ralph Dean Cole believes that "[whatever] he may write together with what he has already written will make better . . . thinkers of those who read and study him."[70] We can agree with Juan Soler Planas, who maintains that the combination of Marías's philosophical ability and his literary style has produced many long-lasting ideas that should contribute to the modernization of Christian philosophy and the Christianization of modern philosophy.[71]

The overall assessment by Marías himself of his many literary endeavors is that the most interesting aspect of them is their unity. Despite the fact that he has treated a great number of topics throughout his long career as a writer, "those which reality has been presenting me," he has done so—he thinks—from a philosophical perspective that consists in seeing precisely the *reality* that each of these themes possesses, grounding them in "my life." "And I believe that the literary style in which all this is written, articulated in a plurality of genres, is also essential."[72] We could not agree more. Never have we read a philosopher more conscious of his literary style, which ultimately means of how well his readers will understand him through the instrument he uses to express his ideas. Likewise, never have we read a philosopher more aware of the necessity of being systematic, which refers to the cognitive apprehension of the actual connections in lived reality. The combination of these two is rare, and we believe there is reason to be enthusiastic in discovering them. By this point it should be obvious that we are especially enthusiastic about Marías's presentation of the empirical structure of human life on earth, seeing it as a fertile source of further philosophical inquiry. Our hope is that his philosophical contribution will be discovered and critiqued by an ever larger audience.

Notes and References

Chapter One

1. Julián Marías, "Carta abierta," in *Obras* (Madrid, 1966), 7:434. It appeared originally as the prologue, under the title of "Carta abierta al estudiante americano," in *Modos de vivir: Un observador español en los Estados Unidos*, ed. Edward R. Mulvihill and Roberto G. Sánchez, (New York, 1964). Hereafter all references are to works by Marías unless otherwise noted.

2. Ibid., pp. 436–37.

3. "La experiencia de la vida," in ibid., p. 648; English in *Philosophy as Dramatic Theory* (University Park, Pa., 1971), p. 298. Cf. "El 'fracaso' del liberalismo" and "El contenido del liberalismo," in *Innovación y arcaísmo* (Madrid, 1973), pp. 228–35; *Meditaciones sobre la sociedad española*, *Obras* (Madrid, 1970), 8:249–51; and *España en nuestras manos* (Madrid, 1978), p. 249 where he writes: "During some twenty years, if I was not the only liberal [in Spain], I believe I have been the only practicing one who was active and publicly so. And I will continue to be such, if others like it or not."

4. Julián Marías and Germán Bleiberg, *Diccionario de literatura española*, 3d ed. (Madrid: Revista de Occidente, 1964), p. 307.

5. This is the title of the reedited version of 1963; the original edition of 1944 appeared under the title of *La preocupación de España en su literatura*.

6. *Antropología metafísica* (Madrid, 1970), pp. 209–10; italics his; English in *Metaphysical Anthropology* (University Park, Pa., 1971), p. 178. Cf. *La mujer en el siglo xx* (Madrid, 1980).

7. *Meditaciones sobre la sociedad española*, in *Obras*, 8:237 ff.

8. Cecilia Silva, "Entervista con Julián Marías," Soria, Spain, August 5, 1977. This portion was omitted from the printed interview in *Hispania* 61 (1978): 365–68.

9. "Ante la constitución," in *España en nuestras manos*, pp. 209–49.

10. *Consideración de Cataluña*, in *Obras*, 8:387. Cf. ibid., p. 384.

11. *España en nuestras manos*, p. 240.

12. Ibid., p. 120. My brief account of the transition from dictatorship to

democracy in Spain does not mean the situation was simple and free from factional infighting. For a detailed account, cf. Raymond Carr and Juan Pablo Fusi Aizpurua, *Spain: Dictatorship to Democracy* London, 2nd ed., 1981). Marías is mentioned several times in the study, on one occasion being referred to as an "incurable optimist."

13. "La realidad histórica y social del uso lingüístico," in *Obras*, 8:656. Insofar as writing can be considered a profession, it does not—according to Marías—coincide completely with who he is. *La mujer en el siglo xx.* pp. 81–82.

14. *La España real* (Madrid, 1976), p. 287.

15. *Consideración de Cataluña*, in *Obras*, 8:413. For an account of the conditions of censorship for the anti-Franco writers who refused to emigrate, cf. Paul Ilie, *Literature and Inner Exile, Authoritarian Spain, 1939–1975* (Baltimore, 1980). The study refers to the Mead-Marías controversy on the state of intellectual life in Francoist Spain.

16. "Treinta años de vida intelectual," in *Innovación y arcaísmo*, p. 17.

17. Ibid.

18. Silva, p. 366b.

19. *La mujer en el siglo xx.* p. 85.

20. *Introducción a la filosofía*, in *Obras* (Madrid, 1962), 2: xxi; English in *Reason and Life, The Introduction to Philosophy* (New Haven, 1956), p. vii.

21. "En la muerte de Ortega. Ortega: historia de una amistad," in *Obras* (Madrid, 1960), 5:378. The lecture Ortega delivered that day can be read in chapter 1 of *Unas lecciones de metafísica* (Madrid, 1966); English translation in *Some Lessons in Metaphysics* (New York, 1969). The lecture constitutes the most beautifully phrased introduction to philosophy known to this writer. Cf. "Encuentro con Ortega," in *Obras* (Madrid, 1959), 3:85–87; originally published as the prologue to Miguel Ramis Alonso, *En torno al pensamiento de José Ortega y Gasset* (Madrid, 1948).

22. Ibid., p. 379.

23. Cf. *La escuela de Madrid*, in *Obras*, vol. 5., especially "Zubiri o la presencia de la filosofía," pp. 465–73 and "La situación intelectual de Xavier Zubiri," pp. 474–80, as well as "El legado filosófico de Manuel García Morente," pp. 459–64. Also, cf. "La escuela de Madrid," in *Historia de la filosofía* (Madrid, 1978), pp. 449–55; English in *History of Philosophy* (New York, 1967), pp. 462–68. *Historia de la filosofía* was dedicated "to the memory of my teacher Manual García Morente who was dean and guiding spirit of that Faculty of Philosophy and Letters where I was introduced to philosophy."

24. "Prólogo," in *Ortega: I. Circunstancia y vocación* (Madrid, 1960), p. 27; English in *José Ortega y Gasset, Circumstance and Vocation* (Norman, 1970), p. 10.

25. Ibid., p. 27; English, p. 11.

26. Ibid., English, p. 10.

27. "Prólogo a las ediciones americana y inglesa," in *Introducción a la filosofía*, in *Obras*, 2: xxiii; English in *Reason and Life*, p. ix.

28. "Prólogo," in *Ortega: Circunstancia y vocación*, pp. 27–28; English in *José Ortega y Gasset, Circumstance and Vocation*, p. 11.

29. Ibid., p. 28; English, p. 11.

30. José Luis Pinillos, "Prólogo," in *La visión responsable, La filosofía de Julián Marías* by Harold C. Raley, (Madrid, 1977), p. 9.

31. Enrique Lafuente Ferrari, "Compás," in *Nuestra Andalucía*, in *Obras*, 8:428.

32. "Gregorio Marañón," in *Obras*, 7:164.

33. *España real*, p. 159.

34. "Preface to the American Edition," in *Miguel de Unamuno* (Cambridge, Mass., 1966), pp. viii–ix.

35. *Miguel de Unamuno*, in *Obras*, 5:25–27; English in *Miguel de Unamuno*, pp. 8–10.

36. "En la muerte de Ortega. Ortega: historia de una amistad," in *Obras*, 5:381.

37. Ibid.

38. "En la muerte de Ortega. El hombre Ortega," in *Obras*, 5:392.

39. "La psiquiatría vista desde la filosofía," in *Obras*, (Madrid, 1959), 4:347–63; English in "Psychiatry from the Point of View of Philosophy," in *Philosophy as Dramatic Theory*, pp. 141–63; and "La estructura corpórea de la vida humana," in *Obras*, 8:602–18; English in "The Corporeal Structure of Life," in ibid., pp. 165–88.

40. *Antropología metafísica*, pp. 87–89; English in *Metaphysical Anthropology*, pp. 72–74. I have chosen to follow the lead of Frances Lopéz-Morillas, the English translator of *Metaphysical Anthropology*, in rendering *sexuado* into the neologism "sexuate." To translate the word into "sexed," as did James Parsons in "The Corporeal Structure of Human Life," does not sufficiently emphasize Marías's distinction between *having* sex organs (*sexual*) and *being* of one sex or the other in all dimensions of human living (*sexuado*).

Chapter Two

1. *Introducción a la filosofía*, in *Obras*, 2:11; English in *Reason and Life*, p. 12. This use of "radical" in its literal meaning of "root" or fundamental has its source in Ortega, whose clearest explanation is seen in his *El hombre y la gente* in *Obras*, 7:99. English in *Man and People* (New York, 1963), p. 38.

2. Ibid., pp. 13–14; English, p. 14.

3. Ibid., p. 7; English, p. 7.

4. *Historia de la filosofía*, in *Obras* (Madrid, 1958), 1:5; English in *History of Philosophy*, p. 5.

5. "La filosofía griega desde su origen hasta Platón," in *Biografía de la*

filosofía, in *Obras,* 2:429; An English translation, by Harold C. Raley, will be published soon.

6. Ibid., p. 535.

7. "Los dos cartesianismos," in *Ensayos de teoría,* in *Obras,* 4:457. This essay will be chapter 10 of the expanded edition in the English translation of *Biografía de la filosofía.*

8. "La filosofía de la vida," in *Biografía de la filosofía,* 2:623.

9. "La escolástica en su mundo y en el nuestro," in ibid., p. 535.

10. *Antropología metafísica,* p. 16; English in *Metaphysical Anthropology,* p. 8.

11. Ibid.

12. "La estructura dramática de la teoría filosófica," in *Nuevos ensayos de filosofía,* in *Obras,* 8:497; English in "The Dramatic Structure of Philosophic Theory," in *Philosophy as Dramatic Theory,* p. 54.

13. *Idea de la metafísica,* 2:406; English in *The Idea of Metaphysics* in *Contemporary Spanish Philosophy: An Anthology,* ed. A. Robert Caponigri, (Notre Dame, Ind., 1967), p. 361.

14. Ibid., p. 407; English, p. 362.

15. "La estructura dramática de la teoría filosófica," in *Obras,* 8:490; English in *Philosophy as Dramatic Theory,* pp. 44–45.

16. *Introducción a la filosofía,* in *Obras,* 2:363, n. 1; English in *Reason and Life,* p. 399, n. 1. Reference is to José Ortega y Gasset, *Obras Completas* (Madrid: Revista de Occidente, 1961), 6:406.

17. *Idea de la metafísica,* in *Obras,* 2:412; English in Caponigri, p. 369.

Chapter Three

1. *Idea de la metafísica,* in *Obras,* 392; English in Caponigri, p. 352.

2. Ibid.

3. *Antropología metafísica,* p. 89; English in *Metaphysical Anthropology,* p. 74.

4. Ibid., p. 255; English, p. 218.

5. Ibid., p. 97; English, p. 80.

6. Ibid., p. 105; English, p. 88.

7. *España en nuestras manos,* p. 263.

8. Ibid.

9. *Antropología metafísica,* p. 165; English in *Metaphysical Anthropology,* p. 138.

10. Ibid., pp. 189–90; English, p. 160.

11. Ibid., p. 192; English, p. 163.

12. Ibid., p. 187; English, p. 158.

13. Ibid., p. 190; English, pp. 160–61.

14. Ibid., p. 214; English, pp. 181–82.

15. Ibid., pp. 218, 219, 231; English, pp. 185, 186, 196.

16. *La mujer en el siglo xx,* p. 229.

17. Ibid., pp. 209, 235.

18. *Antropología metafísica*, pp. 288–89; English in *Metaphysical Anthropology*, p. 248.

19. Ibid., p. 299; English, p. 257 (italics in original). Cf. "La 'Meditatio Mortis,' tema de nuestro tiempo," in *Nuevos ensayos de filosofía*, in *Obras*, 8:539–48; English in "Meditatio Mortis—Theme of Our Times," in *Philosophy as Dramatic Theory*, pp. 117–30.

20. Ibid., pp. 308–9; English, p. 267 (italics mine).

Chapter Four

1. This distinction was developed by Ortega in his incomplete series of lectures in 1949–1950 at the Institute of Humanities, published posthumously (1957) as *El hombre y la gente*, in *Obras Completas* (Madrid: Revista de Occidente, 1961), 7:71–271; English translation, *Man and People* (New York: Norton, 1963).

2. *Introducción a la filosofía*, in *Obras*, 1:233; English in *Reason and Life*, p. 257.

3. Ibid., p. 235; English, p. 259.

4. Willard R. Trask translates *vigencias* as "observances" in *Man and People*, while Harold C. Raley retains the original Spanish in his translation of *Generations, A Historical Method*. We have chosen to translate it as "binding observances," emphasizing the power of observances to force us to comply.

5. *La estructura social*, in *Obras*, 6:171.

6. Ibid., p. 179.

7. "El problema de las generaciones en el siglo XIX," in *El método histórico de las generaciones*, in *Obras*, 6:18–56. English in "The Problem of Generations in the Nineteenth Century," in *Generations, A Historical Method* (University, Alabama, 1970), pp. 18–68.

8. "Las vicisitudes del tema en nuestro siglo," in ibid., pp. 84–114; English translation in "The Vicissitudes of the Generation Theme in Our Century," pp. 105–56.

9. "La teoría de Ortega," in ibid., pp. 84–114; English translation in "The Theory of Generations of Ortega," pp. 69–106.

10. *La estructura social*, in *Obras*, 6:189 (italics in original).

11. Ibid., p. 191.

12. Cf. "Cervantes y las generaciones" and "Azorín y las generaciones," in *Literatura y generaciones* (Madrid, 1975), pp. 9–24, 133–38. For a discussion of the literary generation of 1936, including Marías, see: Helio Carpintero. "Los ensayistas contemporáneos," *Ínsula* 224–25, (February 1965): 11, 30.

13. "El método histórico," in *El método histórico de las generaciones*, in *Obras*, 6:129–43; English translation in "The Historical Method," in *Generations, A Historical Method*, pp. 170–88. For a reference to the age of

woman, relative to man, within a generation, see: *La mujer en el siglo xx*, p. 83.

14. *La estructura social, Obras*, 6:206.

15. "Generaciones augustos y césares," in *Literatura y generaciones*, p. 179.

16. *Ortega: Circunstancia y vocación*, p. 144; English in *José Ortega y Gasset, Circumstance and Vocation*, p. 127.

17. *La estructura social*, in *Obras*, 6:219.

18. José Ortega y Gasset, "Ideas y creencias,"in *Obras Completas* (Madrid: Revista de Occidente, 1961), 5:375.

19. *La estructura social*, in *Obras*, 6:350.

20. "La lengua española como instalación histórica," in *España en nuestras manos*, pp. 277–85. Cf. "La realidad histórica y social del uso lingüístico," in *Obras*, 8:619–56, which constitutes Marías's inaugural address before the Spanish Royal Academy on 20 June 1965, and "La sociedad y la lengua," *Consideración de Cataluña*, in ibid., pp. 358–62. For a comment on Marías's presentation in the Academy, see: *Insula* 224–25 (February 1965): 2.

Chapter Five

1. *Análisis de los Estados Unidos*, in *Obras*, 8:15; English in *America in the Fifties and Sixties: Julián Marías on the United States* (University Park, Pa., 1972), p. 267.

2. "From Spain," in *As Others See Us, The United States through Foreign Eyes*, ed. Franz M. Joseph, (Princeton, 1959), p. 55. As far as we can discover, this essay was never published in the Spanish original.

3. Carlos A. del Real, Julián Marías, and Manuel Granell, *Juventud en el mundo antiguo: Crucero universitario por el Mediterráneo* (Madrid, 1934), p. 207. Those who organized the trip judged the diary of del Real to be the most complete expression of the essential aspects of the trip, which included Tunisia (Kairouan), Malta, Egypt (Alexandria, Cairo, and the Pyramids at Giza), Palestine (Jaffa, Jerusalem, Bethlehem, the Dead Sea area, and Tel Aviv), Crete, Rhodes, Turkey (Constantinople), Greece (Athens, Nauplion, Delphi, and Mt. Olympus), and Italy (Syracuse and Palermo in Sicily, and Naples and Pompeii on the mainland). It was decided to publish the complete diary of the winner, along with excerpts from those of two others. Granell's was chosen as the best exposition of the contents of the trip, while Marías's was included as the most expressive personal reflection on the things seen.

4. Ibid., p. 222.

5. Ibid., p. 232.

6. Ibid., p. 238.

7. Ibid., p. 252.

8. *Consideración de Cataluña*, in *Obras*, 8:393.

9. José Ortega y Gasset, *Meditaciones del Quijote, Commentario por Julián Marías* (Madrid: Revista de Occidente, 1957), p. 129. Marías's commentary is on pp. 366–67; English in *Meditations on Quixote* (New York: Norton, 1963), p. 103.

10. *Ortega: Circunstancia y vocación,* p. 389 (italics in original); English in *José Ortega y Gasset, Circumstance and Vocation,* p. 365.

11. "El extranjero y el turista," in *Obras,* 6:511.

12. "Plaza Mayor," in *Obras* (Madrid: Revista de Occidente, 1959), 3:344 ff. Cf. "La magia de los nombres," in *Obras,* 6:463; and "Hispanoamerica: 'dramatis personae,' " ibid., pp. 456 ff.

13. Silva, p. 367b.

14. "¿Naciones?" and "Sobre naciones," in *Ensayos de convivencia,* in *Obras,* 3:332–33, 334–38.

15. "Puerto Rico después de 1898: Lo que ha ganado. Lo que ha perdido," in *Meditaciónes sobre la sociedad española,* in *Obras,* 8:314–21.

16. "Carta abierta," in *Obras,* 8:437.

17. "From Spain," in *As Others See Us, The United States through Foreign Eyes,* ed. Joseph, p. 25.

18. *Miguel de Unamuno,* p. ix of English. As far as we can discover, this was never published in Spanish.

19. "La proa," in *Análisis de los Estados Unidos,* in *Obras,* 8:134–37; English in "The Prow," in *America in the Fifties and Sixties: Julián Marías on the United States,* pp. 410–14.

20. "Carta abierta," in *Obras,* 8:438.

21. Cf. "Spanish and American Images," in *Foreign Affairs,* 39 (1960–1961): 92–99; "From Spain," in Joseph, pp. 25–56; and "The Spaniard" in "Spain Today," *Atlantic* 207 (1961): 73–76.

22. *Los Estados Unidos en escorzo,* in *Obras,* 3:353 (italics in original); English in *America in the Fifties and Sixties: Julián Maritas on the United States,* p. 15. Also, cf. "From Spain," in Joseph, p. 44. Europe, for Marías, must always be seen in the context of the West. Indeed, he considers himself a citizen of the West, his true fatherland. See: *La mujer en el siglo xx,* p. 97.

23. "From Spain," in Joseph, p. 29.

24. *Imagen de la India,* in *Obras,* 8:195–234.

25. *Israel: Una resurreción,* in *Obras,* 8:141–91. Spain had still not recognized Israel by the time Spanish television ran the American series on the "Holocaust." The presentation was preceded by a 75-minute round-table discussion by four Spaniards on the devastation of European Jewry. According to the report in the *New York Times,* 30 June 1979: "They resolutely skirted Franco's treatment of Jews during the Nazi period. Comparing Hitler's Germany and medieval Spain, Julián Marías, a philosopher and essayist, gamely offered that in Spain Jews were at least given a chance to convert to Christianity 'or leave the country.' "

26. Cf. "La mitad femenina," "La amistad en Norteamérica," "Nuestra

cuidad," and "Soledad juntas," in *Los Estados Unidos en escorzo*, in *Obras*, 3:458–66, 523–25, 381–83, 384–86; English in "The Feminine Half of the U.S.A.," "Friendship in North America," "Our City," and "A Cluster of Solitudes," in *America in the Fifties and Sixties: Julián Marías on the United States*, pp. 148–59, 228–31, 48–51, 51–54.

27. "La televisión," in ibid., pp. 484–88; English, pp. 181–86.

28. *Israel: Una resurrección*, in *Obras*, 8:184. Cf. "El estilo y su ausencia," in *Ensayos de convivencia*, in *Obras*, 3:339–443.

29. "La 'town' y el 'surburb,'" in *Análisis de los Estados Unidos*, in *Obras*, 8:76, 77; English in "Town and Suburb," in *America in the Fifties and Sixties: Julián Marías on the United States*, p. 341.

30. "Cuzco en tres tiempos," in *Ensayos de convivencia*, in *Obras*, 3:328.

31. "La cuidad invertebrada," in *Los Estados Unidos en escorzo*, in *Obras*, 3:507–11; English in "The Invertebrate City," in *America in the Fifties and Sixties: Julián Marías on the United States*, pp. 207–13.

32. *Consideración de Cataluña*, in *Obras*, 8:339–422. Cf. "Cataluña veinte años después," in *Obras*, 3:224–27. This series of essays arose from a motor trip Marías made through the region in September and October 1965, having been invited by the newspaper *El noticero universal* of Barcelona, in whose pages the fifteen articles were first published. For a reaction to the essays, cf. Maurici Serrahima, *Realidad de Cataluña, Respuesta a Julián Marías* (Barcelona, 1967).

Nuestra Andalucía, in *Obras*, 8:425–79. This book was born of much observation in that region over a period of many years, almost from Marías's childhood. The proximate occasion was a study trip organized by Dorothy Mulberry in May and June 1965 for twelve coeds from Mary Baldwin College. The essays, first printed in a Barcelona newspaper, arose from long conversations had during the trip on what was seen and experienced. Enrique Lafuente Ferrari, Marías's former professor of art history at the University of Madrid, accompanied them as a teacher (and wrote the introduction), as did Alfredo Ramón, whose watercolors illustrated the original edition published in 1966 by Diaz Casariego of Madrid.

33. "La realidad regional," in *Consideración de Cataluña*, in *Obras*, 8:384 (italics in original).

34. "La catalanización de Barcelona," in ibid., pp. 273–74. Cf. "Behold Iberia," in *This Land of Europe: A Photographic Exploration* by Dennis Stock (Tokyo, 1976), p. 124. Originally written in English by Marías, a Spanish translation by him appeared in: *Gaceta ilustrada*, 12 August 1979.

35. "El catalán como posibilidad," in *Consideración de Cataluña*, in *Obras*, 8:363–67.

36. *Meditaciónes sobre la sociedad española*, in *Obras*, 8:256.

37. "Formas estéticas y formas de vida," in *Consideración de Cataluña*, in *Obras*, 8:368.

38. Ibid.

39. Ibid., p. 371.

40. "Cataluña veinte años después," in *Obras*, 3:226. Marías mentions the book by José Ferrater Mora entitled *Las formas de la vida catalana* (1943).

41. "Behold, Iberia," in *This Land of Europe*, p. 122.

42. "La casa enjalbegada," in *Nuestra Andalucía*, in *Obras*, 8:434.

43. "La España nunca vista," in *Obras*, 8:270. This is the title of the prologue written for *Sobre la piel del toro* (Barcelona, 1965), p. 6. This unique work of aerial photographs of Spain was published in four volumes: (1) *Tierras y paisajes*, by Pierre Deffontaines; (2) *España histórica y monumental*, by Luis Monreal y Tejada; (3) *España moderna*, by Luis Romero; and (4) *España en fiestas*, by Luis Romero.

44. "Entre la Andalucía trágica y la Andalucía prospera," in *Nuestra Andalucía*, in *Obras*, 8:469.

Chapter Six

1. "El tiempo de la ficción," in *La imagen de la vida humana*, in *Obras*, 5:525.

2. "El lugar de la literatura en la educación," in *Literatura y generaciones*, p. 204.

3. Ibid., p. 198.

4. "La 'Meditatio Mortis,' tema de nuestro tiempo," in *Obras*, 8:539–48; English in " 'Meditatio Mortis,'—Theme of Our Time" in *Philosophy as Dramatic Theory*, pp. 117–30.

5. "El sentido metódico de la novela" in *Miguel de Unamuno*, in *Obras*, 5:74; English in "The Significance of the Novel as Method," in *Miguel de Unamuno*, p. 65.

6. "La estructura dramática de la teoría filosófica," in *Obras*, 8:494; English in "The Dramatic Structure of Philosophical Theory," in *Philosophy as Dramatic Theory*, p. 50.

7. "Los géneros literarios en filosofía," in *Obras*, 4:317; English in "Literary Genres in Philosophy," in *Philosophy as Dramatic Theory*, p. 18.

8. Ibid., pp. 330–31; English, pp. 20–21.

9. Ibid., p. 335; English, p. 27.

10. Ibid., pp. 338–39; English, p. 31. Portion inserted between ellipsis is from "El lugar de la literatura en la educación," in *Literatura y generaciones*, p. 199.

11. "Philosophic Truth and the Metaphoric System" in *Interpretations: The Poetry of Meaning*, eds. S. R. Hopper and D. L. Miller, (New York, 1967), p. 45. Originally written in English by Marías. Like Ortega, Marías does not favor neologisms, using them sparingly, one example of which is *solencias*, Cf. *La mujer en siglo xx*, p. 92.

12. Ibid., p. 47.

13. Ibid., p. 48.

14. Ibid., p. 52.

15. Ibid., pp. 52–53.

16. "El teatro y la representación," in *La imagen de la vida*, in *Obras*, 5:538.

17. "El tiempo de la ficción," in ibid., p. 528.

18. "La realidad humana en la novela," in ibid., p. 531.

19. Ibid., p. 532.

20. "El tiempo de la ficción," in ibid., p. 526.

21. "Nuestra imagen de la vida," in ibid., pp. 569–70.

22. "El teatro y la representación," in ibid., p. 535.

23. "Nuestra imagen de la vida," in ibid., p. 566.

24. "Realidad histórica y social del uso lingüístico," in *Obras*, 8:655.

25. *Ensayos de convivencia*, p. 155; quoted in Ralph Dean Cole, *Julián Marías as Literary Critic* (Ann Arbor: University Microfilms International, 1977), p. 86.

26. "El mundo cinematográfico," in *La imagen de la vida humana*, in *Obras*, 5:550.

27. "La pantalla," in ibid., p. 545.

28. *Visto y no visto* (Madrid, 1970), 1:542.

29. Ibid., pp. 16–17.

Chapter Seven

1. "La filosofía actual y el ateísmo," in *Obras*, 8:525; English in "Contemporary Philosophy and Atheism," in *Philosophy as Dramatic Theory*, pp. 97–98.

2. "Realidad histórica y social del uso lingüístico," in *Obras*, 8:655. Cf. *Ortega: Circunstancia y vocación*, p. 264; English in *José Ortega y Gasset, Circumstance and Vocation*, p. 247.

3. José Angeles, Review of *Al margen de los clásicos*, *Books Abroad* 41 (1967): 449a.

4. James H. Abbott, Review of *Israel: Una resurrección: Imagen de la India*, ibid., 45 (1971); 87a–b and Review of *Nuevos ensayos de filosofía*, ibid., 44 (1970): 85.

5. As reported in Cole, pp. 79–80.

6. Hans Beerman, Review of *El tiempo que ni vuelve ni tropieza*, *Books Abroad* 39 (1965): 332b.

7. *Ortega: Circunstancia y vocación*, p. 266; English in *José Ortega y Gasset, Circumstance and Vocation*, p. 248.

8. "El estilo y su ausencia," in *Obras*, 3:342.

9. Beejee Smith, "Prologue," in *Al margen de estos clásicos* (Madrid, 1967): 18, 8.

10. Cf. "El ensayo en España," in *Los Españoles*, in *Obras*, 7:166–69, to see Marías's view that this genre is the most frequently used in Spain. We have not been able to locate his early essay "Cuatro posturas ante el ensayo," *La estafeta literaria* 15 (1944): 21. Also, cf. "Ensayo y novela," in *Ensayos de convivencia*, in *Obras*, 3:243–49.

11. "Los géneros literarios en filosofía," in *Obras*, 4:339; English in "Literary Genres in Philosophy," in *Philosophy as Dramatic Theory*, p. 32.

12. Ibid., p. 338; English, p. 31.

13. Cf. Paul G. Kuntz, "The Dialectic of Historicism and Antihistoricism," *Monist* 53 (1969): 656–69, for the state of the controversy.

14. In the essay on "Psychiatry from the Point of View of Philosophy" (1952) he says this level has not been studied. Cf. "La psiquiatría vista desde la filosofía," in *Obras*, 4:356; English in *Philosophy as Dramatic Theory*, p. 154. However, in *Metaphysical Anthropology* (1970), he says "classical philosophy did not find the theme *entirely* alien." (*Antropología metafísica*, p. 89 [italics in original]; English, p. 74.) The implication is that nobody has treated it as he intends to do so.

15. *Antropología metafísica*, p. 124; English in *Metaphysical Anthropology*, p. 104.

16. Ibid., p. 94; English, p. 78.

17. Cf. James L. Christian, ed., *Extra-Terrestrial Intelligence: The First Encounter* (Buffalo: Prometheus Books, 1976). Of the fifteen contributors, seven are professional philosophers, including the editor. The most valuable contribution from our perspective is that on "Would ETI's be Persons?" by Michael Tooley, former professor of philosophy at Stanford University and presently a full-time research scholar at the Research School of Social Sciences at the Australian National University. This interest apparently grew out of his previous attempts to establish criteria for judging whether or not a living thing is a person, as in cases involving ethical issues dealing with abortion, euthanasia, and the right to die.

18. Ibid., p. 4. Bradbury is a science-fiction writer himself. The anthology also includes Issac Asimov, a biochemist who received a Hugo Award (1963) for "putting the science in science fiction."

19. Science Fiction Research Association, Annual Conference, 22–24 June 1979, South Lake Tahoe, California, and Popular Culture Association Convention, 18–21 April 1979, Pittsburgh.

20. *Antroplogía metafísica*, p. 117; English in *Metaphysical Anthropology*, p. 97. Cf. "La psiquiatría vista desde la filosofía," in *Obras*, 4:357; English in "Psychiatry from the Point of View of Philosophy," in *Philosophy as Dramatic Theory*, p. 154. See also *La mujer en el siglo xx*, p. 142.

21. Ibid., p. 240; English, p. 204.

22. Maryellen MacGuigan, "Is Woman a Question?," *International Philosophical Quarterly* 13 (1973): 504. The other contemporary thinkers whose positions on woman MacGuigan examines are José Ortega y Gasset, Karl Stern, and F. J. Buytiendijk.

23. Ibid.

24. *Antropología metafísica*, p. 196; English in *Metaphysical Anthropology*, pp. 166–67.

25. *La mujer en el siglo xx*, p. 95.

26. *Solencias* is a neologism introduced by Marías, despite the fact that he has very little attraction for the coining of new terms, to refer to negative

usages that are not prohibitions in the strict sense of forbidding an expressed action. When such usages are broken, society is "surprised" at the "insolence" of the offender. As Marías views it, women have been surrounded by such negative binding observances throughout all of history. Cf. *La mujer en el siglo xx*, p. 92.

27. José Luis Pinillos, "Prólogo" in Harold C. Raley, *La visión responsable, La filosofía de Julián Marías* (Madrid: Espasa-Calpe, 1977), p. 26.

28. Mario Parajón, "Autobiografía metafísica," *Revista de Occidente* 117 (1972): 404.

29. Joseph Rubin, unpublished paper.

30. "From Spain," Joseph, p. 56.

31. Ibid.

32. Ibid.

33. Michael Aaron Rockland, introduction to *America in the Fifties and Sixties: Julián Marías on the United States*, p. 6.

34. Robert Merton, "Introducción a un libro de Marías," *Revista de Occidente* 148 (1975): 107. On subjectivity and objectivity in sociology, cf. Deena Weinstein and Michael A. Weinstein, "An Existential Approach to Society: Active Transcendence," *Human Studies* 1 (1978): 1–10.

35. *La estructura social, Obras*, 6:252–53.

36. Rockland, pp. 9–10.

37. Russell Kirk, "Perceptions like Tocqueville's," *Yale Review* 62 (1972): 147.

38. Cf. "La burocracia como una forma de satanismo," in *Los Estados Unidos en escorzo*, in *Obras*, 3:512–14; English in "Bureaucracy as a Form of Satanism," in *America in the Fifties and Sixties: Julián Marías on the United States*, pp. 214–17. Cf. Russell Kirk, "Ultimate Bureaucracy: Is Satan in the Computer?," *Detroit News*, 30 October 1972.

39. Howard T. Young, Review of *Los Estados Unidos en escorzo, Books Abroad* 31 (1957): 258.

40. William McCann "A Spanish Tocqueville Today," *University Bookman* 13 (1972): 86.

41. Ibid., p. 89.

42. Ibid.

43. Juan López-Morillas, *Intelectuales y espirituales* (Unamuno, Machado, Ortega, Marías, Lorca) (Madrid: Revista de Occidente, 1961), p. 249.

44. Durant Da Ponte, "The Spanish Image of America," *Hispania* 47 (1964): 113.

45. Young, p. 258a.

46. Robert E. Lott, Review of *Análisis de los Estados Unidos, Books Abroad* 42 (1968): 560–61.

47. "Universidad y sociedad en los Estados Unidos," in *Los Estados Unidos en escorzo*, in *Obras*, 3:416; English in "The University and Society in the United States," in *America in the Fifties and Sixties: Julián Marías on the United States*, p. 93.

48. "La filosofía en Yale," in ibid., p. 430; English in "Philosophy at Yale," p. 112.

49. "Carta abierta," in *Obras*, 7:437. Marías himself acknowledged it was difficult to render his motto into English. After discussing it with various friends in the United States and in Madrid, Marías suggested the various translations. Mulvihill and Sánchez translate it as "I do my part," as does Raley for the English edition of his *La visión responsable, La filosofía de Julián Marías.*

50. Michael A. Weinstein, unpublished paper on Marías's liberalism.

51. Ibid.

52. "La filosofía actual y el ateísmo," in *Obras*, 8:530–31; English in "Contemporary Philosophy and Atheism," in *Philosophy as Dramatic Theory*, p. 105.

53. Arthur Goodfriend, "The Cognoscenti Abroad—V: Julián Marías's Madrid," *Saturday Review* 52 (14 June 1969): 39. Marías was Goodfriend's guide through Madrid and, in pointing out the city he loves, revealed himself and his likes, including his participation in "talks" (*tertulias*) and his pastime of collecting old books.

54. Cf. "La filosofía actual y el ateísmo," in *Obras*, 8:530; English in "Contemporary Philosophy and Atheism," in *Philosophy as Dramatic Theory*, p. 104; and "La escolástica en el mundo actual," in *Biografía de la filosofía*, in *Obras*, 2:554–69.

55. Cf. "La filosofía actual y el ateísmo," in *Obras*, 8:531. English in "Contemporary Philosophy and Atheism," in *Philosophy as Dramatic Theory*, p. 106. *Antroplogía metafísica*, p. 308; English in *Metaphysical Anthropology*, p. 266.

56. Cf. chapter 4, "De fide et ratione," "Constitutio dogmatica de fide catolica" of First Vatican Council, 1869–1870, as seen in *Enchiridion Symbolorum*, ed. Karl Rahner (Rome: Herder, 1960), no. 1795, pp. 495–96. The belief is based on Romans, 1, 20, which states that God is known through created things. For Aquinas's proofs for the existence of God, see Etienne Gilson, *The Christian Philosophy of St. Thomas Aquinas* (New York: Random House, 1956), pp. 59–83, and for the metaphysical basis for these proofs, see Etienne Gilson, *Being and Some Philosophers* (Toronto: Pontifical Institute of Mediaeval Studies, 1952).

57. "Presencia y ausencia del existencialismo en España," in *La escuela de Madrid*, in *Obras*, 5:217; English in "The Presence and Absence of Existentialism in Spain," *Philosophy and Phenomenological Research* 15 (1954–55): 180. (Marías was quoted favorably by Marcel in his Gifford Lectures of 1949: Gabriel Marcel, *The Mystery of Being*, vol. 1, *Reflection and Mystery* [Chicago: Henry Regnery, 1960], p. 100.) On the other hand, Etienne Gilson, a Thomist as renowned as Maritain, told this author in the late 1950s of his shock to discover, upon a visit to Spain, that the teaching of Scholasticism was a prerequisite in Spain for holding a teaching position in philosophy.

Spanish Scholastics have denied that Marías has an adequate understanding of Scholasticism. Cf. Juan Roig Gironella, "Revista de *Introducción a la filosofía*," *Pensamiento* 4 (1948): 16. For Marías's response to Roig Gironella's critique of Ortega, see *Ortega y tres antípodas* (Buenos Aires: Revista de Occidente, 1950), pp. 94–99. It is interesting to note that the book was not published by Revista de Occidente in Spain but in Argentina. Perhaps the censors refused their permission, as they had to Marías's critique of "official" philosophy in Spain in his "Dios y césar: unas palabras sobre Morente," in *Ensayos de convivencia*, in *Obras*, 3:143–50.

58. *La estructura social*, in *Obras*, 4:207.

59. Ciriaco Morón Arroyo, *El sistema de Ortega y Gasset* (Madrid: Ediciones Alcalá, 1968), pp. 417–38.

60. José Luis Abellán, "Panorama de la filosofía española," *Razón y fe* 947 (1977): 140. There is no mention of Marías in Luis Martínez Gómez, "Filosofía español actual," *Pensamiento* 29 (1973): 347–65, although his *Antropología metafísica* must have been one of the works the author had in mind when speaking of Ortega's influence on metaphysical anthropology. Cf. Círico Flórez Miguel, "Panorama de la vida filosófica en España hoy," Serafín Tabernos del Rio, "Actitudes ante Ortega," and Enrique Rivera de Ventosa, "La evolución del pensamiento eclesiástico de España (1939–1975)," in *Actas del I seminario de historia de la filosofía española* (Salamanca, 1978), pp. 119–44, 253–64, 275–91.

61. *Tres visiones de la vida humana* (Madrid, 1972). The edition contains "La imagen de la vida humana," "La experiencia de la vida," and "Idea de la metafísica."

62. Edward Sarmiento, "The Mind of Julián Marías. A Catholic Disciple of Ortega," *Tablet* 197, no. 5 (30 June 1951): 516a. Cf. Edward Sarmiento, "Orteguianismo y cristianismo," *Atlante* 3 no. 4 (1955): 167–70.

63. "La idea de la vida en Dilthey," in *Biografía de la filosofía*, *Obras*, 2:619.

64. *Introducción a la filosofía*, *Obras*, 2:110; English in *Reason and Life*, p. 122.

65. Quoted by Marías in *Ortega: Circunstancia y vocación*, pp. 268–69. English translation in *José Ortega y Gasset, Circumstance and Vocation*, p. 251. It was published originally in Ortega, "Intimidades. La pampa . . . promesas," in *Obras Completas* (Madrid: Revista de Occidente, 1961), 2:636. The reference is mistakenly given as page 630 in both the Spanish original and the English translation of Marías's work. The "saving" is to be understood in conjunction with his statement in *Meditations on Quixote* of "saving" our circumstances, of giving meaning to them.

66. *Miguel de Unamuno*, *Obras*, 5:201; English in *Miguel de Unamuno*, p. 213.

67. Harold C. Raley, *La visión responsable. La filosofía de Julián Marías*, p. 367; English in *Responsible Vision: The Philosophy of Julián Marías* (Clear Creek, Indiana: American Hispanist, 1980), p. 320.

68. Helio Carpintero, *Cinco aventuras españolas* (Ayala, Laín, Aranguren, Ferrater, Marías) (Madrid: Revista de Occidente, 1967), p. 201.

69. López-Morillas, pp. 245, 249–50.

70. Cole, p. 102.

71. Juan Soler Planas, *El pensamiento de Julián Marías* (Madrid: Revista de Occidente, 1973), p. 239. This was Soler Planas's doctoral dissertation, under the direction of Nemesio González Caminero, S.J., at the Pontifical Gregorian University in Rome. The fifth chapter is on critical reflections and contains a sympathetic evaluation of Marías's metaphysics from the Thomistic perspective. González Caminero considers Marías to be one of the "enthusiastic disciples" of Ortega, along with Pedro Laín Entralgo, José Luis López Aranguren, Luis Díez del Corral, and José Antonio Maravell, none of whom have denounced or diminished their Catholic faith. Cited in Soler Planas, p. 227, n. 41.

72. Letter from Julián Marías to Antón Donoso, 24 May 1979.

Bibliography

PRIMARY SOURCES

1. Works

Obras Madrid: Revista de Occidente, 1958–1970. **vol. 1:** *História de la filosofía* (1941; 10th ed., 1958, in *Obras*); **vol. 2:** *Introducción a la filosofía* (1947); *Idea de la metafísica* (1954); *Biografía de la filosofía* (1954); **vol. 3:** *Aquí y ahora* (1954); *Ensayos de convivencia* (1955); *Los Estados Unidos en escorzo* (1956); **vol. 4:** *San Anselmo y el insensato* (1944); *La filosofía del Padre Gratry* (1941); *Ensayos de teoría* (1954); *El intelectual y su mundo* (1956); **vol. 5:** *Miguel de Unamuno* (1943); *La escuela de Madrid* (1959); *La imagen de la vida humana* (1956); **vol. 6:** *El metódo histórico de las generaciones* (1949); *La estructura social* (1955); *El oficio del pensamiento* (1958); **vol. 7:** *Los españoles* (1962); *La España posible en tiempo de Carlos III* (1963); *El tiempo que ni vuelve ni tropieza* (1964); **vol. 8:** *Análisis de los Estados Unidos* (1968); *Israel: Una resurreción* (1968); *Imagen de la India* (1961); *Meditaciones sobre la sociedad española* (1966); *Consideración de Cataluña* (1966); *Nuestra Andalucía* (1966); *Nuevos ensayos de filosofía* (1968).

Al margen de los clásicos: Autores españoles del siglo xx. Madrid: Afrodisio Aguado, 1967. Prologue and glossary by Beejee Smith.

Antropología metafísica: La estructura empírica de la vida humana. Madrid: Revista de Occidente, 1970.

La devolución de España. Madrid: Espasa-Calpe, 1977.

España en nuestras manos. Madrid: Espasa-Calpe, 1978.

La España real. Madrid: Espasa-Calpe, 1976.

"Ferrater y su diccionario." *Ínsula* 148 (1959): 3.

"La idea del estado latente en el método de Menéndez Pidal." *Ínsula* 141 (1958): 3, 8.

Innovación y arcaísmo. Madrid: Revista de Occidente, 1973.

La justicia social y otras justicias. 1973, 2d ed. Madrid: Espasa-Calpe, 1979.

Literatura y generaciones. Madrid: Espasa-Calpe, 1975.

Meditaciones de Quijote: Comentario. Madrid: Revista de Occidente, 1957.

Modos de vivir: Un observador español en los Estados Unidos. New York: Oxford University Press, 1964. Selections from the writings of Marías edited by Edward R. Mulvihill and Roberto G. Sánchez.

La mujer en el siglo xx. Madrid: Alianza Editorial, 1980.

"Notas de un viaje a Oriente." In *Juventud en el mundo antiguo: Crucero universitario por el Mediterráneo,* by Carlos A. del Real, Julián Marías, and Manuel Granell, pp. 191–254. Madrid: Espasa-Calpe, 1934.

Ortega: Circunstancia y vocación. [Vol. 1] Madrid: Revista de Occidente, 1960.

Ortega y tres antípodas: Un ejemplo de intriga intelectual. Buenos Aires: Revista de Occidente, 1950.

"Prólogo." In *Diarios,* by Gaspar Melchor de Jovellanos. Madrid: Alianza, 1967.

Problemas del cristianismo. Madrid: Biblioteca de Autores Cristianos, 1979.

"La realidad humana en la novela." *Universidad de Antioquia,* 31 (1955): 391–95.

"La retracción a España del europeo Ortega. Hace sesenta años," *Revista de Occidente* 140 (1974): 181–95.

"Salvador de Madariaga (1886–1978)," *Boletín de la Real Academia Española,* 59 (1979), 19–25.

"Sobre la *Política* de Aristóteles." *Revista de Estudios Políticos* 55 (1951): 63–73.

"La teoria de la inducción en Gratry." *Cuadernos Hispanoamericanos* 18 (1954): 143–61.

"Una jornada muy particular," *Gaceta ilustrada,* January 15, 1978.

Valle Inclán en el ruedo ibérico. Buenos Aires: Columba, 1967.

Visto y no visto. 2 vols. Madrid: Guadarrama, 1970.

"La vocación occidental de los Estados Unidos." *Revista de Occidente* 12 (1976): 24–29.

2. Collaborations

Diccionario de literatura española. 3d ed. Madrid: Revista de Occidente, 1964. With Germán Bleiberg.

Historia de la filosofía y de la ciencia. Madrid: Guadarrama, 1964. With Pedro Laín Entralgo.

3. Translations (listed in alphabetical order of author translated)

ARISTOTLE. *Etica a Nicomaco.* Madrid: Instituto de Estudios Políticos, 1960. In collaboration with María Araujo.

―――. *Política.* Madrid: Instituto de Estudios Políticos, 1951. In collaboration with María Araujo.

BÜHLER, KARL. *Teoría del lenguaje*. Madrid, 1950.

COMTE, AUGUSTE. *Discurso sobre el espíritu positivo*.

DILTHEY, WILHELM. *Introducción a las ciencias del espíritu*. Madrid: Revista de Occidente, 1956.

————. *Teoría de las concepciones del mundo*. Madrid: Revista de Occidente, 1944.

GRATRY, ALPHONSE. *El conocimiento de Dios*. Madrid: Pegaso, 1941.

HAZARD, PAUL. *La crisis de la conciencia europea (1680–1715)*. Madrid: Pegaso, 1941.

————. *El pensamiento europeo en el siglo xviii*. Madrid, 1946.

HÖPKER-ASCHOFF, HERMANN. *El dinero y el oro*. Madrid: Revista de Occidente, 1940.

KANT, IMMANUEL. "Sobre el concepto de la filosofía en general." *Ideas y valores* 9–10 (1954): 83-87.

————. *Sobre el saber filosófico*.

LEHMANN, R. *Introducción a la filosofía*. Buenos Aires: Losada, 1941

LEIBNIZ, WILHELM. *Discurso de metafísica*. Madrid: Revista de Occidente, 1942.

MAINE DE BIRAN, PIERRE. "La existencia de un estado puramente afectivo." *Revista de Psicología General y Aplicada* 2 (1947): 227-39.

SCHELER, MAX. *De lo eterno en el hombre: La esencia y los atributos de Dios. Madrid*, 1940.

SPRANGER, EDUARD. *Cultura y educación*. Buenos Aires, 1948.

TURGOT, A. R. J.. "Existencia." *Revista Psicología General y Aplicada* 3 (1948): 705, 729.

4. Anthologies

La filosofía en sus textos. 2 vols. Barcelona: Labor, 1950. 3 vols. Barcelona: Labor, 1963.

Obras selectas de Miguel de Unamuno. 1st ed. Madrid: Pléyade, 1946.

El tema del hombre. Madrid: Revista de Occidente, 1943. Abridged ed., Madrid: Espasa-Calpe, 1952.

5. English Translations (essays originally written in English by Marías indicated by an asterisk)

"America and Spain." *Américas* 24 (February 1972): 13-18.

America in the Fifties and Sixties: Julián Marías on the United States. Edited by Michael Aaron Rockland, translated by Blanche De Puy and Harold C. Raley. University Park, Pa.: Pennsylvania State University Press, 1971.

°"Behold, Iberia." *This Land of Europe: A Photographic Exploration*, by

Dennis Stock. Introduction by H. R. Trevor-Roper. Tokyo: Kodansha International, 1976. Pp. 117-24. Distributed in the United States through Harper & Row. Spanish translation by Marías to be found in *Gaceta ilustrada*, 12 August 1979.

"Contemporary Spain in World Culture." *Cahiers d'Historie Mondiale* 6 (1960-1961): 1006-22.

Don Quixote as Seen by Sancho Panza. Basavangudi, Bangalore: Indian Institute of Culture, 1956.

"From Spain." Translated by James F. Shearer. In *As Others See Us, The United States through Foreign Eyes*. Edited by Franz M. Joseph. Princeton: Princeton University Press, 1959, Pp. 25-56.

"Generation." In *International Encyclopedia of the Social Sciences*, edited by David L. Sills, 6:88-92. New York: Macmillan & The Free Press, 1968.

Generations: A Historical Method. Translated by Harold C. Raley. University, Ala.: University of Alabama Press, 1971.

History of Philosophy. Translated by Stanley Applebaum and Clarence C. Stowbridge. New York: Dover, 1966.

"The Idea of Metaphysics." Translated by A. Robert Caponigri. In *Spanish Philosophy, An Anthology*. Edited by A. Robert Caponigri. Notre Dame: University of Notre Dame, 1967. Pp. 324-370.

"Indian Sketchbook." *Commonweal* 72 (27 May 1960): 226-227.

José Ortega y Gasset: Circumstance and Vocation. Translated by Frances M. López-Morillas. Norman: University of Oklahoma Press, 1970.

"Latin America and the Flying Buttress Policy." *Americas* 22 (May 1970): 16-20.

Metaphysical Anthropology: The Empirical Structure of Human Life. Translated by Frances M. López-Morillas. University Park, Pa.: Pennsylvania State University Press, 1971.

Miguel de Unamuno. Translated by Frances M. López-Morillas. Cambridge: Harvard University Press, 1966.

"Ortega and the Idea of Vital Reason." *Dublin Review* 222-23 (1949): 56-79, 36-54.

°"Philosophic Truth and the Metaphoric System." In *Interpretation: The Poetry of Meaning*, edited by S. R. Hopper and D. L. Miller, Pp. 41-51. New York: Harcourt, Brace and World, 1967.

Philosophy as Dramatic Theory. Translated by James D. Parsons. University Park, Pa.: Pennsylvania State University Press, 1971.

"The Presence and Absence of Existentialism in Spain." Translated by Janet Aronson Weiss. *Philosophy and Phenomenological Research* 15 (1954-1955): 180-91.

"Prologue for American Readers" and "Introduction" [plus "the most essential" notes from his commentary on the Spanish edition of Ortega's *Meditaciones del Quijote*]. In *Meditations on Quixote*, by José

Ortega y Gasset. Translated by Evelyn Rugg and Diego Marín. New York: Norton, 1963.

Reason and Life: The Introduction to Philosophy. Translated by Kenneth S. Reid and Edward Sarmiento. New Haven: Yale University Press, 1956.

"Reflections on Poverty." *Commonweal* 74 (11 August 1961): 439–41.

"The Situation of the Intelligentsia in Spain Today." *Daedalus* 89 (1960): 622–31.

"Spain Is in Europe." *Books Abroad* 26 (1952): 233–36.

"The Spaniard." In "Spain Today." *Atlantic* 207 (1961): 73–76.

°"Spanish and American Images." *Foreign Affairs* 39 (1960–1961): 92-99.

"Suárez." *Dublin Review* 221 (1948): 115–30.

"Toward a Philosophy of the Armed Forces." *Americas* 24 (October 1972): 25-27.

"Two Indias." *Commonweal* 71 (22 January 1960): 459–61.

"The United States in 1974." Translated by James H. Abbott. *Norman* [Oklahoma] *Transcript,* 2–6 February 1975.

°"Unreal America." *Foreign Affairs* 39 (July 1961): 578–90.

SECONDARY SOURCES

ABELLÁN, JOSÉ LUIS. "De cultura y filosofía española (II): Julián Marías y Manuel Granell." *Ínsula* 287 (1970): 10. This is really two standard book reviews, one following the other, the only connection being that both writers have been influenced by Ortega. It is listed merely because the title gives an indication of more than a standard review. (No standard review is listed in this section, only those that are review-essays.) The book by Marías reviewed is *Antropología metafísica.* Of special interest is Abellán's contention that Ortega would not agree with Marías's interpretation of metaphysics. On line 13 of column "b" is found a typographical error, with "empirical" where "analytical" should be, or (which is unlikely) Abellán misunderstood Marías's position.

BASH, LINDA C. "The Social Structure of the United States in the Works of Julián Marías." M.A. thesis, Bowling Green State University, 1971. An application of the "abstract" sociological categories of *La estructura social* to Marías's essays on the United States, thus "concretizing" them. An excellent idea for a thesis, admirably executed. It should be published.

BOLINGER, DWIGHT L. ". . . And Should Thereby Be Judged," *Books Abroad* 27 (1953): 129–32. A reply to Marías's response to an article by Robert G. Mead, Jr., "Dictatorship and Literature in the Spanish World," *Books Abroad* 25 (1951): 223-26, deploring the ill effects of the dictatorships of Franco and Perón on the intellectual orientation of the Spanish world. Marías's response, "Spain Is in Europe," *Books Abroad*

26 (1952): 233-36, affirmed that much healthy intellectual life was still going on in Spain. Bolinger points out that Marías missed the point, that even in his and Bleiberg's *Diccionario de literatura española* certain names that should have been listed are omitted because of the unfavorable political circumstances.

CARPINTERO CAPELL, HELIO. *Cinco aventuras españoles: Araguren, Ayala, Ferrater, Laín, Marías.* Madrid: Revista de Occidente, 1968. Pp. 191-233. Deals with Marías's notion of philosophy and its history as leading to a knowledge of man—with reference to Unamuno and Ortega and the Spanish intellectual scene.

―――. "Los ensayistas contemporáneos." *Ínsula* 224-25 (1965): 30. Discusses the generation of 1936 in Spain, including Marías.

COLE, RALPH DEAN. *Julián Marías as a Literary Critic.* Ann Arbor: University Microfilms International, 1977. Cole's doctoral dissertation for the University of Oklahoma (1974). Excellent synthesis of all Marías has written from the perspective of literary criticism. It should be published.

FERRATER MORA, JOSÉ. "Marías (Julián)." In *Diccionario de filosofía.* 5th ed. Buenos Aires: Sudamericana, 1971. 1:136-37. Brief overview that emphasizes Marías's contributions to philosophy as his theory of empirical structure of human life and his idea of metaphysics.

GOODFRIEND, ARTHUR. "The Cognoscenti Abroad—V: Julián Marías's Madrid." *Saturday Review* 52 (14 June 1969): 39-41. A delightfully written picture of Madrid through Marías's eyes, showing his love of the city as he escorted Goodfriend around.

GUY, ALAIN. "Julián Marías." In *Les Philosophes Espagnols D'Hier et D'Aujourd'Hui: Epoques et auteurs.* Toulouse: Privat, 1956. Pp. 330-39. General presentation of Marías's position. Guy points out that Marías is a friend of France, speaking French perfectly.

KIRK, RUSSELL. "Perceptions Like Tocqueville's." *Yale Review* 62 (1972): 142-47. An essay-review of the English translation of Marías's essays on the United States, comparing him favorably with Tocqueville.

LÓPEZ QUINTAS, ALFONSO. "La lógica de la rázon vital." *Filosofía española contemporánea.* Madrid: Biblioteca de Autores Cristianos, 1970. Pp. 164-74. Brief presentation of Marías's position, followed by excerpts from some of his works.

LÓPEZ-MORILLAS, JUAN. *Intelectuales y espirituales. Unamuno, Machado, Ortega, Marías, Lorca.* Madrid: Revista de Occidente, 1961. Essay-reviews of first three volumes of Marías's *Obras*, originally published in *Papels de Son Armandans* 43 (1959): 61-88.

McINNES NEIL. "Marías, Julián." In *Encyclopedia of Philosophy*, edited by Paul Edwards, New York: Macmillan & The Free Press, 1967. 5:160. Brief treatment (one half of a page) giving impression that Marías is primarily interested in religion. States (incorrectly) that Ortega was "explicitly irreligious and anti-Catholic."

MERTON, ROBERT. "Introducción a un libro de Marías." *Revista de Occidente* 148 (1975): 99-111. The Spanish translation of Merton's "Introduction" to the forthcoming English translation of Marías's *La estructura social* as *The Structure of Society*. Very complimentary, especially showing that Marías is not "subjectivistic" in his method.

MORTIZ, CHARLES. ed. "Marías (Aguilera), Julián." *Current Biography Yearbook, 1972*. New York: H. W. Wilson, 1972. Pp. 308-10. An excellent overview, including many references to book reviews.

MULVIHILL, EDWARD R. and SÁNCHEZ, ROBERTO G. "Introduction." In *Modos de vivir: Un observador español en los Estados Unidos*. New York: Oxford University Press, 1964. Pp. ix–xiii. Brief biographical sketch of Marías for the American student of Spanish, for whom the anthology is intended.

PARAJÓN, MARIO. "Autobiografía metafísica." *Revista de Occidente* 117 (1972): 387-405. Essay-review of *Antropología metafísica* that briefly elaborates on some of the book's points.

PINILLOS, JOSÉ LUIS. "Prólogo." In *La visión responsable, La filosofía de Julián Marías*, by Harold C. Raley. Translated by César Armando Gómez. Madrid: Espasa-Calpe, 1977. Pp. 9-27. An interesting treatment, with personal aspects, of Marías's reputation in Spain.

RAAHAUGE CAMAGNA, MARIANGELA. "Julián Marías e l'Europa" and "Julián Marías: Unamuno e la Spagna." *Filosofia* (Torino) 23 (1972): 157-64, 239-54. Excerpts from Raahauge Camagna's doctoral dissertation for the University of Torino, the first article dealing with Marías's notion of Europe and the second with his treatment of Spain.

RALEY, HAROLD C. "Hacia una teoría estética en Julián Marías." *Hispanófila* 41 (1970): 55-59. Sketch of Marías's aesthetics from scattered references to the subject. An excellent introduction.

————. "Julián Marías: Hacia la superación de Ortega." *Hispanófila* 35 (1969): 45-50. Shows how Marías is correct in saying he is irreducible to Ortega.

————. "Translator's Preface." In *Generations: A Historical Method*. University, Ala.: University of Alabama Press, 1967. Pp. vii–xi. Provides an excellent context for *El método histórico de las generaciones*.

————. *La visión responsable. La filosofía de Julián Marías*. Translated by César Armando Gómez. Madrid: Espasa-Calpe, 1977. An excellent and most sympathetic treatment concentrating on human life, preceded by an examination of the influence of Ortega and Unamuno on Marías. English version: *Responsible Vision: The Philosophy of Julián Marías*. Clear Creek, Indiana: American Hispanist, 1980.

RAMIREZ, O.P., SANTIAGO. *La zona de seguridad: "Rencontre" con el último epígono de Ortega*. Salamanca: San Esteban, 1959. An answer to Marías's charge that the attacks of Father Ramírez, then the "dean of Spanish Scholasticism," on Ortega were "dangerous from the point of view of religion." Ramírez continues his earlier criticism that Ortega is incompatible with Catholicism and religion, using St. Thomas Aquinas's philosophy to offset Ortega's position.

ROCKLAND, MICHAEL AARON. "Introduction." Translated by Blanche De Puy and Harold C. Raley. In *America in the Fifties and Sixties: Julián Marías on the United States*. University Park, Pa.: Pennsylvania State University Press, 1972. Pp. 1-11. An excellent overview of the book, a translation of the two sets of essays Marías wrote on the United States.

SARMIENTO, EDWARD. "The Mind of Julián Marías." *Tablet* 197 (30 June 1951): 515-17. Attempts to show Ortega's thought is not incompatible with Catholicism. (The *Tablet* is one of England's leading Catholic publications.)

SERRAHIMA, MAURICI. *Realidad de Cataluña: Respuesta a Julián Marías*. Barcelona: Aymá, 1967. A generally most favorable reaction to Marías's *Consideración de Cataluña*.

SILVA, CECILIA. "Entrevista con Julián Marías" [Soria, España, 5 de agosto de 1977]. *Hispania* 61 (1978): 365-68. Reveals Marías's attitudes toward Spanish culture, including its manifestation in Spanish America. (The published version is much reduced from the original.)

SMITH, BEEJEE. "Prologue." In *Al margen de estos clásicos: Autores españoles del siglo xx*, Madrid: Afrodisio Aguado, 1967. Pp. 7-19. Overview of Marías's life and work for students who will use the text.

SOLER PLANAS, JUAN. *El pensamiento de Julián Marías*. Madrid: Revista de Occidente, 1973. Soler Planas's doctoral dissertation for the Gregorian University (Rome), treating Marías's metaphysics, epistemology, and anthropology. He considers Marías's relationship with Ortega in depth. Contains sympathetic criticism from the point of view of Thomism.

VILAR, SERGIO. "Julián Marías and the Intelligentsia in Spain." *Books Abroad* 37 (1963): 252-60. A follow-up of the Mead-Marías controversy, with the author showing great admiration for Marías, but dissenting with him on the issue of the immediate post-Civil War attitude in Spain toward Spanish writers who had gone into exile. Disagrees with Mead that Spanish culture is finished. Very revealing of conditions in Spain during the early years of the dictatorship.

ZANCANARO, PAUL. "Human Life and the Sexuate Condition as Disjunctive." M.A. thesis, University of Windsor (Canada), 1981. An in depth examination of Marías's conception of the sexuate condition as disjunctive within the context of the analytical and empirical structures of human life. His extensive observations, which should be published, introduce an important distinction between ontological equality and socio-political equality in assessing Marías's contention that the relation of the sexes is one of inequality.

Index